65 PICKLES
CHUTNEYS & RELISHES

65 PICKLES
CHUTNEYS & RELISHES

Make your own mouthwatering preserves with
step-by-step recipes and over 230 superb photographs

Catherine Atkinson

southwater

This edition is published by Southwater,
an imprint of Anness Publishing Ltd, Hermes House, 88–89 Blackfriars Road, London SE1 8HA;
tel. 020 7401 2077; fax 020 7633 9499

www.southwaterbooks.com; www.annesspublishing.com

If you like the images in this book and would like to investigate using them for publishing, promotions or
advertising, please visit our website www.practicalpictures.com for more information.

UK distributor: Book Trade Services; tel. 0116 2759086; fax 0116 2759090; uksales@booktradeservices.com;
exportsales@booktradeservices.com
North American distributor: National Book Network; tel. 301 459 3366; fax 301 429 5746; www.nbnbooks.com
Australian distributor: Pan Macmillan Australia; tel. 1300 135 113; fax 1300 135 103; customer.service@macmillan.com.au
New Zealand distributor: David Bateman Ltd; tel. (09) 415 7664; fax (09) 415 8892

Publisher: Joanna Lorenz
Managing Editor: Linda Fraser
Project Editor: Emma Clegg
Jacket Design: Balley Design
Production Controller: Bessie Bai
Photographer: Craig Robertson
Home Economist: Sarah O'Brien
Stylist: Helen Trent

ETHICAL TRADING POLICY
Because of our ongoing ecological investment programme, you, as our customer, can have the pleasure and reassurance of
knowing that a tree is being cultivated on your behalf to naturally replace the materials used to make the book you are holding.
For further information about this scheme, go to www.annesspublishing.com/trees

Previously published as part of these larger volumes: *Preserves* and *Perfect Pickles, Chutneys and Relishes*

PUBLISHER'S NOTE
Although the advice and information in this book are believed to be accurate and true at the time of going to press, neither the
authors nor the publisher can accept any legal responsibility or liability for any errors or omissions that may be made nor for any
inaccuracies nor for any harm or injury that comes about from following instructions or advice in this book.

NOTES
Bracketed terms are intended for American readers. Medium (US large) eggs are used unless otherwise stated.
For all recipes, quantities are given in both metric and imperial measures and, where appropriate, measures are also given in
standard cups and spoons. Follow one set, but not a mixture, because they are not interchangeable.
Standard spoon and cup measures are level.
1 tsp = 5ml, 1 tbsp = 15ml, 1 cup = 250ml/8fl oz
Australian standard tablespoons are 20ml. Australian readers should use 3 tsp in place of 1 tbsp for measuring small quantities.
This book has been written with the reader's safety in mind, and the advice, information and instructions are intended to be clear and safe
to follow. However, cooking with boiling hot mixtures can be dangerous and there is a risk of burns if sufficient care is not taken. Neither the
author nor the publisher can accept any legal responsibility or liability for any errors or omissions made, or for accidents in the kitchen.

contents

INTRODUCTION   6

EQUIPMENT   8

POTTING AND BOTTLING   10

PICKLES   12

CHUTNEYS   30

RELISHES   48

SAVOURY JELLIES   66

SAUCES AND MUSTARDS   82

INDEX   95

INTRODUCTION

Preserving seasonal fruits and vegetables as pickles, savoury jellies, chutneys and relishes is one of the oldest of culinary arts. Once essential for basic survival, preserving is nowadays more often employed as a tasty and efficient method of storing seasonal vegetables or fruits. It can be done in two ways: by heat sterilization, which destroys enzymes and bacteria, or by creating an environment where contaminants are unable to thrive – by drying, salting, or adding sugar, vinegar or alcohol.

AN AGE-OLD TECHNIQUE

Preserving was one of the earliest skills acquired by man, and it was essential for survival during the cold, dark winter months when fresh food was scarce. Sun and wind were the first natural agents to be used: fruits and vegetables laid out in the hot sun or hung in the wind to dry were found to last longer than fresh produce and were lighter and easier to carry. In colder, damp climates, smoke and fire were used to hasten the drying process.

It wasn't long before early man found that salt was a powerful dehydrator, far more consistent and reliable than the natural elements of sun and wind. Salt soon became a highly prized commodity – so much so that wars were fought over it. In fact, sometimes the salt was more valuable than the food it preserved, hence the saying that something is not worth its salt. Using salt to preserve foods made long-distance travel more possible because produce that had previously been perishable could be taken on board ships for journeys that lasted months and sometimes even years. New settlements were built where it was now feasible for people to both grow and store food.

The preservative properties of vinegar and alcohol were discovered around the same time as those of salt, and people also realized that food could be flavoured at the same time that it was being preserved. Vinegar, which creates an acid environment that contaminants cannot live in, was used throughout the world. Malt vinegars were common in countries where beer was brewed, wine vinegar where vines were grown and rice vinegar became popular in the Far East.

Surprisingly the use of sugar as a preservative wasn't discovered until many centuries later. Cane sugar, brought to Europe by Arab merchants in the 12th century, remained a scarce luxury in the Western world for 400 years. It wasn't until the 16th century, when it was introduced to Europe from the West Indies, that sugar became a sought-after ingredient. Soon the demand for it became so great that it encouraged the rise of colonialism and the slave trade. In the 18th century, beetroot (beet), which had always been enjoyed as a vegetable, began to be cultivated specifically for its sugar content. Eventually sugar became plentiful and cheap, and the liking for sweet preserves started to grow.

It was during the 19th century that preserving really came into its own and was considered to be a skilled craft. Many of the recipes we use today are based on those that first appeared in cookbooks during that era. Housewives took pride in filling capacious larders (pantries) with bottles and jars of

Left: Rich, fruity chutneys were first made in India and became popular in Britain in the 19th century.

PICKLE-MAKING TODAY

Nowadays though, the art of pickling and preserving is coming back into its own, not because food needs to be processed to make it keep for long periods but for reasons of quality and variety. Improved travel and communication have increased knowledge of preserves from around the world and more unusual varieties of fruit, vegetables and flavouring ingredients are now readily available. Many people prefer to make their own preserves instead of buying mass-produced products with artificial flavourings and colourings. The satisfaction that comes from being able to create a unique product is also being rediscovered.

This book shows how to make pickles, chutneys, relishes and other savoury preserves with a collection of over 65 stunning recipes. These traditional and contemporary ideas will prove to be an inspiration and pleasure to both the novice and the experienced pickle-maker.

Above: Bottling vegetables in vinegar both preserves and flavours the food, and is a technique that is used all over the world.

pickles, relishes and chutneys made from fruit and vegetables during the summer and autumn while they were plentiful. These were then enjoyed during the lean winter months to supplement their diet, which consisted mainly of salted meats and root vegetables.

In the 20th century, preserving became less fashionable. Many homes had less storage space and, as the range and use of commercially prepared pickles and relishes increased, huge stocks of home-made preserves were no longer either needed or desirable. Imported produce meant that many fruits and vegetables were available all year round – summer vegetables could be bought in the winter months and citrus fruits never disappeared from grocers' shelves. By the middle of the century, refrigerators could be found in most homes, followed by freezers in the 1960s and '70s. During those decades freezing became the preferred way of preserving fruit and vegetables and the old-fashioned techniques became less popular and were often forgotten.

Above: Nowadays chutneys and pickles are made with a range of ingredients, such as beetroot and tangerine.

EQUIPMENT

While very few specialist items are essential for preserving, having the correct equipment for the job helps to ensure success. You will probably have most of the basic items such as a large heavy pan, weighing scales or calibrated measuring cups, wooden spoons, a vegetable peeler, a chopping board and some sharp knives. However, a few specific items such as a salometer and a jelly bag will prove invaluable. The following are readily available from large department stores and specialist kitchen equipment stores.

PRESERVING PAN

A preserving pan or large, heavy pan is essential for making perfect preserves. It must be of a sufficient size to allow rapid boiling without bubbling over (a capacity of about 9 litres/16 pints/8 quarts is ideal); wide enough to allow rapid evaporation of liquid, so that setting point is reached quickly; and have a thick heavy base to protect the preserve from burning during cooking. A non-corrosive preserving pan such as one made of stainless steel is the best choice for making all types of preserves, but especially for pickles, chutneys and relishes that contain a high concentration of acid.

SUGAR THERMOMETER

Invaluable for cooking preserves to the exact temperature needed for a perfect set. Choose a thermometer that goes up to at least 110°C/ 230°F, and has a clip or a handle that can be attached to the pan, so that it does not slip into the boiling preserve.

JELLY BAG

Used to strain fruit juices from cooked fruit pulp for jelly-making, jelly bags are made from calico, cotton flannel or nylon. Some have their own stands; others have loops with which to suspend the bag.

MUSLIN/CHEESECLOTH

Muslin can be used for making spice, herb or jelly bags. To make a jelly bag, layer three squares of muslin together and tie lengths of string (twine) securely to each corner. Either knot the ends together to hang from a single support, or make four loops so the bag can be suspended on the legs of an upturned stool or chair.

Below: A selection of jars with clamp-top, screw-top or two-piece screw-band lids.

JARS AND BOTTLES

When making pickles, chutneys and relishes, a selection of containers is needed. Clear glass is ideal because it is non-corrosive, you can easily check for trapped air bubbles and it looks very pretty when filled. As well as ordinary jam jars and bottles, there are specialist preserving jars that are designed to be heated to a high temperature. Non-corrosive seals are essential, particularly when potting acidic chutneys and pickles.

Wide-necked jars are crucial for recipes using whole or large pieces of fruit or vegetables, but for most preserves it is better to use several smaller jars than one or two large ones.

PRESERVE COVERS

Waxed paper and cellophane, secured by an elastic band, can be used to cover jellies, but paper and cellophane are not vinegar-proof so are unsuitable for preserves containing vinegar. These should be potted in preserving jars with acid-resistant seals or jam jars with plastic-lined lids.

HYDROMETER

A hydrometer measures the density of sugar syrup and can be used when making a range of preserves, savoury jellies and relishes. The tube is marked from 0 to 40 and measures the point to which the weighted tube sinks. The more sugar a syrup contains, the higher the hydrometer will float in it.

Right: A canelle knife and zester are excellent for paring off thin strips of citrus rind for pickles and relishes.

SALOMETER

This works in the same way as a hydrometer but is used to measure the amount of salt dissolved in brine for pickling. Salometers are marked from 0 to 100.

SIEVES AND COLANDERS

Use nylon, plastic or stainless steel sieves and colanders when straining acidic fruit or preserves.

SLOTTED SPOONS AND SKIMMERS

These are useful for lifting and draining solid ingredients and packing them into jars.

ZESTERS

The cutting edge of a zester has five little holes, which, when pulled firmly across the fruit, remove fine strands of citrus rind, leaving the white pith behind. This is ideal for relishes and chutneys that are flavoured with citrus rind.

CANELLE KNIVES

These have a v-shaped tooth that pares 6mm/¼in strips of peel from fruit and vegetables leaving grooves and creating a striped effect.

GRATERS

Box graters usually have a choice of at least three different surfaces, from fine (for nutmeg and lemon rind) to coarse (for hard fruits and vegetables).

MINCERS/GRINDERS AND FOOD MILLS

Both hand and electric mincers can save a good deal of time and energy when processing large quantities of fruit or vegetables.

GRINDERS

The mortar and pestle is perfect for coarsely grinding small quantities of spices. For larger amounts or when a fine powder is required, use a spice mill or coffee grinder kept solely for that purpose.

Left: A box grater with several different surfaces is useful for preparing fruits, vegetables and spices.

POTTING AND BOTTLING

Make sure you have enough jars and bottles and the correct sterilizing equipment before you start to make any preserve.

CHOOSING CONTAINERS

Pickles made from whole or large pieces of fruit or vegetables should be packed into medium or large jars or bottles with a wide neck. Smooth, pourable sauces or relishes can be stored in narrow-necked bottles, but thicker, spoonable preserves should be packed in jars.

STERILIZING JARS AND BOTTLES

Before potting, it is essential to sterilize jars and bottles to destroy any micro-organisms in containers.

Check jars and bottles for cracks or damage, then wash in hot, soapy water, rinse and turn upside-down to drain. Containers may be sterilized in five different ways: by heating in a low oven, using sterilizing tablets, hot-washing in a dishwasher, immersing in boiling water, or heating in a microwave.

oven method

Stand the containers, spaced slightly apart, on a baking sheet lined with kitchen paper. Rest any lids on top. Place in a cold oven, then heat to 110°C/225°F/Gas ¼ and bake for 30 minutes.

sterilizing tablet method

This method is not suitable for delicately flavoured preserves. Following the instructions on the packet, dissolve the tablets and soak the containers in the sterilizing solution. Drain and dry before use.

Below: Medium, wide-necked jars with plastic-coated screw-top lids are ideal for most preserves.

dishwasher method

Put the containers and lids in a dishwasher and run it on its hottest setting, including drying.

boiling water method

1 Place the containers, open-end up, in a deep pan in one layer.

2 Pour enough hot (but not boiling) water into the pan to cover the containers. Bring the water to the boil and boil for 10 minutes.

3 Leave in the pan until the water stops bubbling, then carefully remove and drain upside-down on a clean dishtowel. Turn the containers upright and leave to air-dry for a few minutes.

4 Immerse lids, seals and corks in simmering water for 20 seconds. (Only ever use corks once.)

microwave method

Follow the microwave manufacturer's instructions and only use for jars that hold less than 450g/1lb and short squat bottles.

1 Half fill the clean jars or bottles with water and heat on full power until the water has boiled for at least 1 minute.

2 Using oven gloves, remove the jars or bottles from the microwave. Carefully swirl the water inside them, then pour it away. Drain upside-down on a clean dishtowel, then turn upright and leave to dry.

Left: Preserves stored in clamp-top and two-piece lidded jars make very attractive gifts.

FILLING JARS AND BOTTLES

Most preserves should be potted into hot containers once they are ready. Savoury jellies with added ingredients such as fresh herbs should be left to cool for 10 minutes until a thin skin forms on the surface. Some preserves, such as fruits bottled in alcohol, are potted when cold rather than hot.

SEALING JARS

Different preserves need to be covered and sealed in different ways. Jellies can be covered with a waxed paper disc and the jar covered with cellophane held in place with an elastic band. Pickled vegetables must be sealed in jars with new rubber seals and vacuum or clamp top lids. Chutneys and pickles should be sealed in jars with vinegar-proof lids.

USING LIDDED JARS

Different types of jars are suitable for different types of preserves. **Screw-top lidded jars** are suitable for most preserves, but uncoated metal lids should be avoided for acidic preserves with vinegar because the lid may corrode. **Two-piece lidded jars** consist of a flat rubber- or plastic-coated lid that fits over the top of the jar and a ring that screws on to the neck of the jar to hold the lid in place. **Clamp-top jars** can be used for any kind of preserve.

FILLING AND SEALING BOTTLES

Bottles are perfect for storing sauces and pourable relishes. They can be stoppered with a sterilized cork, then dipped in wax to seal.

1 Using a ladle and funnel, fill the hot sterilized bottles to within 2.5cm/1in of the top.

2 Soak the corks in very hot water for 3–4 minutes, then push into the tops of the bottles as far as they will go. Gently tap the cork into the bottle using a rolling pin or wooden mallet until the cork is within 5mm/¼in of the top of the bottle. Leave the bottles until they are cold.

3 To seal, dip the top of each bottle in melted candle or sealing wax to coat. Leave to set, then dip a second time.

PRESENTATION

Glass jars and bottles look pretty because they allow you to see the preserve inside. Preserving jars are practical and attractive for savoury preserves, while glazed earthenware pots are good for storing chutneys and mustards.

LABELLING PRESERVES

All preserves should be clearly labelled with the date, the name of the preserve and any special notes.

STORING PRESERVES

Preserves should always be stored in a cool, dark, dry place because exposure to warmth and light will affect their colour and flavour and shorten their shelf-life. Many pickles, chutneys and bottled fruits need time to mature before being used.

pickles

Sharp and sweet, warm and mellow, or hot and piquant – pickles are the magical condiments that can transform simple foods into exhilarating meals. Fresh fruits and vegetables preserved in salt or vinegar and flavoured with spices and herbs make fabulously tasty and aromatic accompaniments to cold meats and cheeses, and go well with many roast meats too. They are simple to make and gloriously varied – each one with its own unique character and taste.

dill pickles

Redolent of garlic and piquant with fresh chilli, salty dill pickles can be supple and succulent or crisp and crunchy. Every pickle aficionado has a favourite type.

Makes about 900g/2lb

INGREDIENTS

20 small, ridged or knobbly pickling (small) cucumbers

2 litres/3½ pints/8 cups water

175g/6oz/¾ cup coarse sea salt

15–20 garlic cloves, unpeeled

2 bunches fresh dill

15ml/1 tbsp dill seeds

30ml/2 tbsp mixed pickling spice

1 or 2 hot fresh chillies

1 Scrub the cucumbers and rinse well in cold water. Leave to dry.

2 Put the measured water and salt in a large pan and bring to the boil. Turn off the heat and leave to cool to room temperature.

3 Using the flat side of a knife blade or a wooden mallet, lightly crush each garlic clove, breaking the papery skin.

4 Pack the cucumbers tightly into one or two wide-necked, sterilized jars, layering them with the garlic, fresh dill, dill seeds and pickling spice. Add one chilli to each jar. Pour over the cooled brine, making sure that the cucumbers are completely covered. Tap the jars on the work surface to dispel any trapped air bubbles.

5 Cover the jars with lids and then leave to stand at room temperature for 4–7 days before serving. Store in the refrigerator.

COOK'S TIP

If you cannot find ridged or knobbly pickling cucumbers, use any kind of small cucumbers instead.

pickled mushrooms with garlic

This method of preserving mushrooms is popular throughout Europe. The pickle is good made with cultivated mushrooms, but it is worth including a couple of sliced ceps for their flavour.

Makes about 900g/2lb

INGREDIENTS

500g/1¼lb/8 cups mixed mushrooms, such as small ceps, brown cap (cremini) mushrooms, shiitake and girolles

300ml/½ pint/1¼ cups white wine vinegar or cider vinegar

15ml/1 tbsp sea salt

5ml/1 tsp caster (superfine) sugar

300ml/½ pint/1¼ cups water

4–5 fresh bay leaves

8 large fresh thyme sprigs

15 garlic cloves, peeled, halved, with any green shoots removed

1 small red onion, halved and thinly sliced

2–3 small dried red chillies

5ml/1 tsp coriander seeds, lightly crushed

5ml/1 tsp black peppercorns

a few strips of lemon rind

250–350ml/8–12fl oz/1–1½ cups extra virgin olive oil

1 Trim and wipe the mushrooms and cut any large ones in half.

2 Put the vinegar, salt, sugar and water in a pan and bring to the boil. Add the bay leaves, thyme, garlic, onion, chillies, coriander seeds, peppercorns and lemon rind and simmer for 2 minutes.

3 Add the mushrooms to the pan and simmer for 3–4 minutes. Drain the mushrooms through a sieve, retaining all the herbs and spices, then set aside for a few minutes more until the mushrooms are thoroughly drained.

4 Fill one large or two small cool sterilized jars with the mushrooms. Distribute the garlic, onion, herbs and spices evenly among the layers of mushrooms, then add enough olive oil to cover by at least 1cm/½in. You may need to use extra oil if you are making two jars.

5 Leave the pickle to settle, then tap the jars on the work surface to dispel any air bubbles. Seal the jars, then store in the refrigerator. Use within 2 weeks.

pickled red cabbage

This delicately spiced and vibrant-coloured pickle is an old-fashioned favourite to serve with bread and cheese for an informal lunch, or to use to accompany cold ham, duck or goose.

Makes about 1–1.6kg/2¼–3½lb

INGREDIENTS

675g/1½lb/6 cups red
  cabbage, shredded

1 large Spanish (Bermuda) onion, sliced

30ml/2 tbsp sea salt

600ml/1 pint/2½ cups red wine vinegar

75g/3oz/6 tbsp light muscovado
  (brown) sugar

15ml/1 tbsp coriander seeds

3 cloves

2.5cm/1in piece fresh root ginger

1 whole star anise

2 bay leaves

4 eating apples

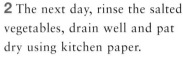

1 Put the cabbage and onion in a bowl, add the salt and mix well until thoroughly combined. Pour the mixture into a colander over a bowl and leave to drain overnight.

2 The next day, rinse the salted vegetables, drain well and pat dry using kitchen paper.

3 Pour the vinegar into a pan, add the sugar, spices and bay leaves and bring to the boil. Remove from the heat and leave to cool.

4 Core and chop the apples, then layer with the cabbage and onions in sterilized preserving jars. Pour over the cooled spiced vinegar. (If you prefer a milder pickle, strain out the spices first.) Seal the jars and store for 1 week before eating. Eat within 2 months. Once opened, store in the refrigerator.

pickled turnips and beetroot

This delicious pickle is a Middle Eastern speciality. The turnips turn a rich red in their beetroot-spiked brine and look gorgeous stacked on shelves in the store cupboard.

2 Put the salt and water in a bowl, stir and leave to stand until the salt has completely dissolved.

3 Sprinkle the beetroot with lemon juice and place in the bottom of four 1.2 litre/2 pint sterilized jars. Top with sliced turnip, packing them in very tightly, then pour over the brine, making sure that the vegetables are covered.

4 Seal the jars and leave in a cool place for 7 days before serving.

Makes about 1.6kg/3½lb

INGREDIENTS

1kg/2¼lb young turnips
3–4 raw beetroot (beets)
about 45ml/3 tbsp coarse sea salt
about 1.5 litres/2½ pints/6¼ cups water
juice of 1 lemon

COOK'S TIP

Be careful when preparing the beetroot because their bright red juice can stain clothing.

1 Wash the turnips and beetroot, but do not peel them, then cut into slices about 5mm/¼in thick.

shallots in balsamic vinegar

These whole shallots, cooked in balsamic vinegar and herbs, are a modern variation on traditional pickled onions. They have a much more gentle, smooth flavour and are delicious served with cold meats or robustly flavoured hard cheeses.

Makes one large jar

INGREDIENTS

500g/1¼lb shallots

30ml/2 tbsp muscovado (molasses) sugar

several bay leaves and/or fresh thyme sprigs

300ml/½ pint/1¼ cups balsamic vinegar

VARIATION

Use other robust herbs in place of the thyme sprigs. Rosemary, oregano or marjoram are all good choices.

1 Put the unpeeled shallots in a bowl. Pour over boiling water and leave to stand for 2 minutes to loosen the skins. Drain and peel the shallots, leaving them whole.

2 Put the sugar, bay leaves and/or thyme and vinegar in a large heavy pan and bring to the boil. Add the shallots, cover and simmer gently for about 40 minutes, or until the shallots are just tender.

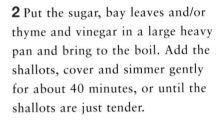

3 Transfer the shallots and vinegar mixture to a warmed sterilized jar, packing the shallots down well. Seal and label the jar, then store in a cool, dark place for about 1 month before eating.

english pickled onions

These powerful, crunchy pickles are traditionally served with a plate of cold meats, bread, cheese and chutney. They should be made with malt vinegar and stored in a preserving jar for at least 6 weeks before eating. Tiny pickling onions are available in the autumn.

Makes about four jars

INGREDIENTS

1kg/2¼lb pickling onions

115g/4oz/½ cup salt

750ml/1¼ pints/3 cups malt vinegar

15ml/1 tbsp sugar

2–3 dried red chillies

5ml/1 tsp brown mustard seeds

15ml/1 tbsp coriander seeds

5ml/1 tsp allspice berries

5ml/1 tsp black peppercorns

5cm/2in piece fresh root ginger, sliced

2–3 blades mace

2–3 fresh bay leaves

1 Trim off the root ends of the onion, but leave the layers. Cut a thin slice off the top (neck) end. Place the onions in a bowl and cover with boiling water. Leave to stand for about 4 minutes, then drain. The skin is then easy to peel with a sharp knife.

2 Place the peeled onions in a bowl and cover with cold water, then drain the water into a large pan. Add the salt and heat slightly to dissolve it, then cool before pouring the brine over the onions.

3 Place a plate inside the top of the bowl and weigh it down slightly so that it keeps all the onions submerged in the brine. Leave to stand for 24 hours.

4 Meanwhile, place the vinegar in a large pan. Wrap all the remaining ingredients, except the bay leaves, in a piece of muslin (cheesecloth). Bring to the boil, simmer for about 5 minutes, then remove the pan from the heat. Set aside and leave to infuse overnight.

5 The next day, drain the onions, rinse and pat dry. Pack them into sterilized 450g/1lb jars. Add some or all of the spice from the vinegar, except the ginger slices. The pickle will become hotter if you add the chillies. Pour the vinegar over to cover and add the bay leaves. (Store leftover vinegar in a bottle for another batch of pickles.)

6 Seal the jars with non-metallic lids and store in a cool, dark place for at least 6 weeks before eating.

stuffed baby aubergines

This Middle Eastern fermented pickle makes a succulent and spicy accompaniment to cold meats, but is equally good served with a few salad leaves and bread as a simple appetizer.

Makes about 3 jars

INGREDIENTS

1kg/2¼lb baby aubergines (eggplant)
2 fresh red chillies, halved lengthways
2 green chillies, halved lengthways
2 celery sticks, cut into matchstick strips
2 carrots, cut into matchstick strips
4 garlic cloves, peeled and finely chopped
20ml/4 tsp salt
4 small fresh vine leaves (optional)
750ml/1¼ pints/3 cups cooled boiled water
45ml/3 tbsp white wine vinegar

2 Steam the slit aubergines for 5–6 minutes or until they are just tender when tested with the tip of a sharp knife.

3 Put the aubergines in a colander set over a bowl, then place a plate on top. Place a few weights on the plate to press it down gently and leave for 4 hours to squeeze out the moisture from the vegetables.

6 Pour the water into a jug (pitcher) and add the remaining 15ml/1 tbsp salt and the vinegar. Stir together until the salt has dissolved. Pour enough brine into the jar to cover the aubergines, then weigh down the top.

7 Cover the jar with a clean dishtowel and leave in a warm, well-ventilated place to ferment. The brine will turn cloudy as fermentation starts, but will clear after 1–2 weeks when the pickle has finished fermenting. As soon as this happens, cover and seal the jar and store in the refrigerator. Eat the pickle within 2 months.

1 Trim the aubergine stems, but do not remove them completely. Cut a slit lengthways along each aubergine, almost through to the other side, to make a pocket.

COOK'S TIPS

• Aubergines come in a multitude of colours from a deep purple-black to yellow and creamy white. Whichever type you use, choose ones with taut, glossy skins.
• Steam the aubergines as soon as you have slit them open because their flesh discolours rapidly when exposed to air.

4 Finely chop two red and two green chilli halves and place in a bowl. Add the celery and carrots to the chillies with the garlic and 5ml/1 tsp of the salt. Mix and use to stuff the aubergine pockets.

5 Tightly pack the aubergines, remaining chillies and vine leaves, if using, into a large sterilized jar.

instant pickle of mixed vegetables

This fresh, salad-style pickle doesn't need lengthy storing so makes the perfect choice if you need a bowl of pickle immediately. However, it does not have good storing properties.

Makes about 450g/1lb

INGREDIENTS

½ cauliflower head, cut into florets

2 carrots, sliced

2 celery sticks, thinly sliced

¼–½ white cabbage, thinly sliced

115g/4oz/scant 1 cup runner (green) beans, cut into bitesize pieces

6 garlic cloves, sliced

1–4 fresh chillies, whole or sliced

5cm/2in piece fresh root ginger, sliced

1 red (bell) pepper, sliced

2.5ml/½ tsp turmeric

105ml/7 tbsp white wine vinegar

15–30ml/1–2 tbsp granulated sugar

60–90ml/4–6 tbsp olive oil

juice of 2 lemons

salt

1 Toss the cauliflower, carrots, celery, cabbage, beans, garlic, chillies, ginger and pepper with salt and leave them to stand in a colander over a bowl for 4 hours.

2 Shake the vegetables well to remove any excess juices.

3 Transfer the salted vegetables to a bowl. Add the turmeric, vinegar, sugar to taste, oil and lemon juice. Toss to combine, then add enough water to distribute the flavours. Cover the bowl and leave to chill for at least 1 hour, or until you are ready to serve.

preserved lemons

Only the rind, which contains the essential flavour of the lemon is used in recipes. Traditionally whole lemons are preserved, but this recipe uses wedges, which can be packed into jars easily.

2 Pack the salted lemon wedges into two 1.2 litre/2 pint/5 cup warmed sterilized jars. To each jar, add 30–45ml/2–3 tbsp sea salt and half the lemon juice, then top up with boiling water to cover the lemon wedges. Seal the jars and leave to stand for 2–4 weeks before using.

3 To use, rinse the preserved lemons well to remove some of the salty flavour, then pull off and discard the flesh. Cut the lemon rind into strips or leave in chunks and use as desired.

Makes about 2 jars

INGREDIENTS

10 unwaxed lemons

about 200ml/7fl oz/scant 1 cup fresh lemon juice or a combination of fresh and preserved juice

boiling water

sea salt

COOK'S TIP

The salty, well-flavoured juice that is used to preserve the lemons can be used to flavour salad dressings or added to hot sauces.

1 Wash the lemons well and cut each into six to eight wedges. Press a generous amount of salt on to the cut surface of each wedge.

pickled plums

This preserve is popular in Central Europe and works well for all varieties of plums, from small wild bullaces and astringent damsons to the more delicately flavoured yellow or red-flushed mirabelle. Plums soften easily, so make sure that you choose very firm fruit.

Makes about 900g/2lb

INGREDIENTS

900g/2lb firm plums

150ml/¼ pint/⅔ cup clear apple juice

450ml/¾ pint/scant 2 cups cider vinegar

2.5ml/½ tsp salt

8 allspice berries

2.5cm/1in piece fresh root ginger, peeled and cut into matchstick strips

4 bay leaves

675g/1½lb/scant 3½ cups preserving or granulated sugar

VARIATION

Juniper berries can be used instead of the allspice berries.

1 Wash the plums, then prick them once or twice using a wooden cocktail stick (toothpick). Put the apple juice, vinegar, salt, allspice berries, ginger and bay leaves in a preserving pan.

2 Add the plums to the pan and slowly bring to the boil. Reduce the heat and simmer gently for 10 minutes, or until the plums are just tender. Remove the plums with a slotted spoon and pack them into hot sterilized jars.

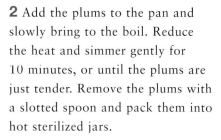

3 Add the sugar to the pan and stir over a low heat until dissolved. Boil steadily for 10 minutes, or until the mixture is syrupy.

4 Leave the syrup to cool for a few minutes, then pour over the plums. Cover and seal. Store for at least 1 month before using and use within 1 year of making.

pickled limes

This hot, pungent pickle comes from the Punjab in India. Salting softens the rind and intensifies the flavour of the limes, while they mature in the first month or two of storage. Pickled limes are extremely salty so are best served with slightly under-seasoned dishes.

Makes about 1kg/2¼lb

INGREDIENTS

1kg/2¼lb unwaxed limes

75g/3oz/⅓ cup salt

seeds from 6 green cardamom pods

6 whole cloves

5ml/1 tsp cumin seeds

4 fresh red chillies, seeded and sliced

5cm/2in piece fresh root ginger, peeled and finely shredded

450g/1lb/2¼ cups preserving or granulated sugar

1 Put the limes in a large bowl and pour over cold water to cover. Leave to soak for 8 hours, or overnight, if preferred.

2 The next day, remove the limes from the water. Using a sharp knife, cut each lime in half from end to end, then cut each half into 5mm/¼in-thick slices.

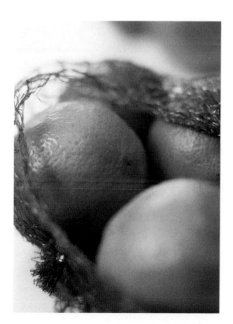

3 Place the lime slices in the bowl, sprinkling the salt between the layers. Cover and leave to stand for a further 8 hours.

4 Drain the limes, catching the juices in a preserving pan. Crush the cardamom seeds with the cumin seeds. Add to the pan with the chillies, ginger and sugar. Bring to the boil, stirring until the sugar dissolves. Simmer for 2 minutes and leave to cool.

5 Mix the limes in the syrup. Pack into sterilized jars, cover and seal. Store in a cool, dark place for at least 1 month before eating. Use within 1 year.

striped spiced oranges

These delightful sweet-sour spiced orange slices have a wonderfully warming flavour and look very pretty. Serve them with baked ham, rich terrines and gamey pâtés. They are also delicious with roasted red peppers and grilled halloumi cheese.

Makes about 1.2kg/2½lb

INGREDIENTS

6 small or medium oranges

750ml/1¼ pints/3 cups white wine vinegar

900g/2lb/4½ cups preserving or granulated sugar

7.5cm/3in cinnamon stick

5ml/1 tsp whole allspice

8 whole cloves

45ml/3 tbsp brandy (optional)

COOK'S TIP

These preserved oranges, with their bright colour and warming flavour, make them a perfect accompaniment during the festive season – delicious with leftover turkey or wafer thin slices of festive ham.

1 Scrub the oranges well, then cut strips of rind from each one using a canelle knife (zester) to achieve a striped effect. Reserve the strips of rind.

2 Using a sharp knife, cut the oranges across into slices slightly thicker than 5mm/¼in. Remove and discard any pips (seeds).

3 Put the orange slices into a preserving pan and pour over just enough cold water to cover the fruit. Bring to the boil, then reduce the heat and simmer gently for about 5 minutes, or until the oranges are tender. Using a slotted spoon, transfer the orange slices to a large bowl and discard the cooking liquid.

4 Put the vinegar and sugar in the cleaned pan. Tie the cinnamon, whole allspice and orange rind together in muslin (cheesecloth) and add to the pan. Slowly bring to the boil, stirring, until the sugar has dissolved. Simmer for 1 minute.

5 Return the oranges slices to the pan and cook gently for about 30 minutes, or until the rind is translucent and the orange slices look glazed. Remove from the heat and discard the spice bag.

6 Using a slotted spoon, transfer the orange slices to hot sterilized jars, adding the cloves between the layers. Bring the syrup to a rapid boil and boil for about 10 minutes, or until slightly thickened.

7 Allow the syrup to cool for a few minutes, then stir in the brandy, if using. Pour the syrup into the jars, making sure that the fruit is completely immersed. Gently tap the jars on the work surface to release any air bubbles, then cover and seal. Store for at least 2 weeks before using. Use within 6 months.

italian mustard fruit pickles

This traditional and popular Italian preserve is made from late summer and autumn fruits,
and then left to mature in time for Christmas when it is served with Italian steamed sausage.

Makes about 1.2kg/2½lb

INGREDIENTS

450ml/¾ pint/scant 2 cups white
  wine vinegar

30ml/2 tbsp mustard seeds

1kg/2¼lb mixed fruit, such as peaches,
  nectarines, apricots, plums, melon,
  figs and cherries

675g/1½lb/scant 3½ cups preserving
  or granulated sugar

VARIATION

If you prefer a slightly less tangy
pickle, use cider vinegar instead of
the white wine vinegar used here.

1 Put the vinegar and mustard
seeds in a pan, bring to the boil,
then simmer for 5 minutes.
Remove from the heat, cover and
leave to infuse for 1 hour. Strain
the vinegar into a clean pan and
discard the mustard seeds.

2 Prepare the fruit. Wash and
pat dry the peaches, nectarines,
apricots and plums, then stone
(pit) and thickly slice or halve
each one of these fruits. Cut the
melon in half, discard the seeds
(pips), then slice into 1cm/½in
pieces or scoop into balls using a
melon baller. Cut the figs into
quarters and remove the stalks
from the cherries.

3 Add the sugar to the mustard
vinegar and heat gently, stirring
occasionally, until the sugar has
dissolved completely. Bring to the
boil, reduce the heat and simmer
for 5 minutes, or until syrupy.

4 Add the fruit to the syrup and
poach it over a gentle heat for
5–10 minutes. Some fruit will be
ready sooner than others, so lift
out as soon as each variety is
tender, using a slotted spoon.

5 Pack the fruit into hot sterilized
jars. Ladle the hot mustard syrup
over the fruit. Cover and seal.
Allow the pickles to mature for at
least 1 month before eating. Use
within 6 months.

blushing pears

As this pickle matures, the fruits absorb the colour of the vinegar, giving them a glorious pink hue. They're especially good served with cold turkey, game pie, well-flavoured cheese or pâté.

Makes about 1.3kg/3lb

INGREDIENTS

1 small lemon

450g/1lb/2¼ cups golden granulated sugar

475ml/16fl oz/2 cups raspberry vinegar

7.5cm/3in cinnamon stick

6 whole cloves

6 allspice berries

150ml/¼ pint/⅔ cup water

900g/2lb firm pears

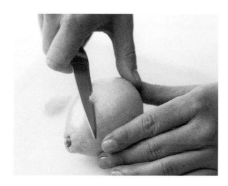

1 Using a sharp knife, thinly pare a few strips of rind from the lemon. Squeeze out 30ml/2 tbsp of the juice and put it in a large pan with the strips of rind.

2 Add the sugar, vinegar, spices and water to the pan. Heat gently, stirring occasionally, until the sugar has completely dissolved, then slowly bring to the boil.

VARIATION

Nectarines and peaches may be pickled using the same method. Blanch and skin the fruits, then halve and stone (pit). Add a strip of orange rind to the syrup instead of lemon rind.

3 Meanwhile, prepare the pears. Peel and halve each one, and then scoop out the cores using a melon baller or small teaspoon. If the pears are of a significant size, cut them into quarters rather than halves.

4 Add the pears to the pan and simmer very gently for about 20 minutes, or until they are tender and translucent but still whole. Check the pears frequently towards the end of the cooking time. Using a slotted spoon, remove the pears from the pan and pack into hot sterilized jars, adding the spices and strips of lemon rind.

5 Boil the syrup for 5 minutes, or until slightly reduced. Skim off any scum, then ladle the syrup over the pears. Cover and seal. Store for at least 1 month before eating.

chutneys

Long, slow cooking produces the classic rich and intriguing flavours that epitomize thick, chunky chutneys. Fresh vegetables and fruits are combined with fresh herbs and spices, then simmered to create wonderfully mellow flavours. These versatile condiments can be served with cold meats and cheeses, or spread thickly in sandwiches to enliven and enhance the simplest fillings.

green tomato chutney

This is a classic chutney for using the last tomatoes of summer that just never seem to ripen. Apples and onions contribute essential flavour, which is enhanced by the addition of spice.

Makes about 2.5kg/5½lb

INGREDIENTS

1.8kg/4lb green tomatoes, roughly chopped

450g/1lb cooking apples, peeled, cored and chopped

450g/1lb onions, chopped

2 large garlic cloves, crushed

15ml/1 tbsp salt

45ml/3 tbsp pickling spice

600ml/1 pint/2½ cups cider vinegar

450g/1lb/2¼ cups granulated sugar

COOK'S TIP

Allow the chutney to mature for at least 1 month before using.

1 Place the tomatoes, apples, onions and garlic in a large pan and add the salt.

2 Tie the pickling spice in a piece of muslin (cheesecloth) and add to the ingredients in the pan.

3 Add half the vinegar to the pan and bring to the boil. Reduce the heat and simmer for 1 hour, or until the chutney is reduced and thick, stirring frequently.

4 Put the sugar and remaining vinegar in a pan and heat gently until the sugar has dissolved, then add to the chutney. Simmer for 1½ hours until the chutney is thick, stirring it occasionally.

5 Remove the muslin bag from the chutney, then spoon the hot chutney into warmed sterilized jars. Cover and seal immediately.

COOK'S TIPS

• To avoid spillages and speed up the process of potting preserves, use a wide-necked jam funnel to transfer the chutney into the jars. Wipe the jars immediately, then label them when cold.

• Use a long-handled teaspoon to press and poke the chutney right down into the pots to exclude any trapped air pockets.

• Press wax discs on the surface of the chutney before sealing the jar.

tomato chutney

This spicy and dark, sweet-sour chutney is delicious served with a selection of well-flavoured cheeses and biscuits or bread, or with cold roast meats such as ham, turkey, tongue or lamb.

Makes about 1.8kg/4lb

INGREDIENTS

900g/2lb tomatoes, skinned
225g/8oz/1½ cups raisins
225g/8oz onions, chopped
225g/8oz/generous 1 cup caster
  (superfine) sugar
600ml/1 pint/2½ cups malt vinegar

VARIATION

Dried dates may be used in place of the raisins, and red wine or sherry vinegar may be used in place of the malt vinegar. Stone (pit) and chop the dates, or buy stoned cooking dates that have been compressed in a block and chop them finely.

1 Chop the tomatoes roughly and place in a preserving pan. Add the raisins, onions and caster sugar.

2 Pour the vinegar into the pan and bring the mixture to the boil. Simmer for 2 hours, uncovered, until soft and thickened.

3 Transfer the chutney to warmed sterilized jars. Top with waxed discs and lids. Store in a cool, dark place and leave to mature for 1 month. The chutney will keep unopened for up to 1 year. Once the jars have been opened, store them in the refrigerator.

mediterranean chutney

Reminiscent of the warm Mediterranean climate, this mixed vegetable chutney is colourful, mild and warm in flavour and goes particularly well with grilled meats and sausages. For a hotter, spicier flavour, add a little cayenne pepper with the paprika.

Makes about 1.8kg/4lb

INGREDIENTS

450g/1lb Spanish (Bermuda) onions, chopped

900g/2lb ripe tomatoes, skinned and chopped

1 aubergine (eggplant), weighing about 350g/12oz, trimmed and cut into 1cm/½in cubes

450g/1lb courgettes (zucchini), sliced

1 yellow (bell) pepper, quartered, seeded and sliced

1 red (bell) pepper, quartered, seeded and sliced

3 garlic cloves, crushed

1 small sprig of rosemary

1 small sprig of thyme

2 bay leaves

15ml/1 tbsp salt

15ml/1 tbsp paprika

300ml/½ pint/1¼ cups malt vinegar

400g/14oz/2 cups granulated sugar

1 Put the chopped onions, tomatoes, aubergine, courgettes, peppers and garlic in a preserving pan. Cover the pan with a lid and cook gently over a very low heat, stirring occasionally, for about 15 minutes, or until the juices start to run.

2 Tie the rosemary, thyme and bay leaves in a piece of muslin (cheesecloth). Add to the pan with the salt, paprika and half the malt vinegar. Simmer, uncovered, for 25 minutes, or until the vegetables are tender and the juices reduced.

3 Add the remaining vinegar and sugar to the pan and stir over a low heat until the sugar has dissolved. Simmer for 30 minutes, stirring the chutney frequently towards the end of cooking time.

4 When the chutney is reduced to a thick consistency and no excess liquid remains, discard the herbs, then spoon the chutney into warmed sterilized jars. Set aside until cool, then cover and seal with vinegar-proof lids.

5 Store the chutney in a cool, dark place and allow to mature for at least 2 months before eating. Use the chutney within 2 years. Once opened, store in the refrigerator and use within 2 months.

confit of slow-cooked onions

This jam of slow-cooked, caramelized onions in sweet-sour balsamic vinegar will keep for several days in a sealed jar in the refrigerator. You can make it with red, white or yellow onions, but yellow onions will produce the sweetest result.

Makes about 500g/1¼lb

INGREDIENTS

30ml/2 tbsp olive oil

15g/½oz/1 tbsp butter

500g/1¼lb onions, sliced

3–5 fresh thyme sprigs

1 fresh bay leaf

30ml/2 tbsp light muscovado (brown) sugar, plus a little extra

50g/2oz/¼ cup ready-to-eat prunes, chopped

30ml/2 tbsp balsamic vinegar, plus a little extra

120ml/4fl oz/½ cup red wine

salt and ground black pepper

3 Add the prunes, vinegar, wine and 60ml/4 tbsp water to the pan and cook over a low heat, stirring frequently, for 20 minutes, or until most of the liquid has evaporated. Add a little more water and reduce the heat if it looks dry. Remove from the heat.

4 Adjust the seasoning if necessary, adding more sugar and/or vinegar to taste. Leave the confit to cool then stir in the remaining 5ml/ 1 tsp olive oil and serve.

VARIATION

Gently brown 500g/1¼lb peeled pickling (pearl) onions in 60ml/4 tbsp olive oil. Sprinkle in 45ml/3 tbsp brown sugar and caramelize a little, then add 7.5ml/1½ tsp crushed coriander seeds, 250ml/8fl oz/1 cup red wine, 2 bay leaves, a few thyme sprigs, 3 strips orange rind, 45ml/3 tbsp tomato purée (paste) and the juice of 1 orange. Cook gently, covered, for 1 hour, stirring occasionally. Uncover for the last 20 minutes. Sharpen with 15–30ml/ 1–2 tbsp sherry vinegar.

1 Reserve 5ml/1 tsp of the oil, then heat the remaining oil with the butter in a large pan. Add the onions, cover and cook gently over a low heat for about 15 minutes, stirring occasionally.

2 Season the onions with salt and ground black pepper, then add the thyme, bay leaf and sugar. Cook slowly, uncovered, for a further 15–20 minutes until the onions are very soft and dark. Stir the onions occasionally during cooking to prevent them sticking or burning.

kashmir chutney

In the true tradition of the Kashmiri country store, this is a typical family recipe passed down from generation to generation. It is wonderful served with plain or spicy grilled sausages.

Makes about 2.75kg/6lb

INGREDIENTS

1kg/2¼lb green eating apples

15g/½oz garlic cloves

1 litre/1¾ pints/4 cups malt vinegar

450g/1lb dates

115g/4oz preserved stem ginger

450g/1lb/3 cups raisins

450g/1lb/2 cups soft light brown sugar

2.5ml/½ tsp cayenne pepper

30ml/2 tbsp salt

COOK'S TIP

This sweet, chunky, spicy chutney is perfect served with cold meats for an informal buffet lunch.

1 Quarter the apples, remove the cores and chop coarsely. Peel and chop the garlic.

2 Place the apple and garlic in a pan with enough vinegar to cover. Bring to the boil and boil for 10 minutes.

3 Chop the dates and ginger and add them to the pan, together with the rest of the ingredients. Cook gently for 45 minutes.

4 Spoon the mixture into warmed sterilized jars and seal immediately.

fiery bengal chutney

Not for timid tastebuds, this fiery chutney is the perfect choice for lovers of hot and spicy food. Although it can be eaten a month after making, it is better matured for longer.

Makes about 2kg/4½lb

INGREDIENTS

115g/4oz fresh root ginger
1kg/2¼lb cooking apples
675g/1½lb onions
6 garlic cloves, finely chopped
225g/8oz/1½ cups raisins
450ml/¾ pint/scant 2 cups malt vinegar
400g/14oz/1¾ cups demerara
  (raw) sugar
2 fresh red chillies
2 fresh green chillies
15ml/1 tbsp salt
5ml/1 tsp turmeric

1 Peel and finely shred the fresh root ginger. Peel, core and roughly chop the apples. Peel and quarter the onions, then slice as thinly as possible. Place in a preserving pan with the garlic, raisins and vinegar.

2 Bring to the boil, then simmer steadily for 15–20 minutes, stirring occasionally, until the apples and onions are thoroughly softened. Add the sugar and stir over a low heat until the sugar has dissolved. Simmer the mixture for about 40 minutes, or until thick and pulpy, stirring frequently towards the end of the cooking time.

3 Halve the chillies and remove the seeds, then slice them finely. (Always wash your hands with soapy water immediately after handling chillies.)

4 Add the chillies to the pan and cook for a further 5–10 minutes, or until no excess liquid remains. Stir in the salt and turmeric.

5 Spoon the chutney into warmed sterilized jars, cover and seal them immediately, then label when cool.

6 Store the chutney in a cool, dark place and leave to mature for at least 2 months before eating. Use within 2 years of making. Once opened, store in the refrigerator and use within 1 month.

butternut, apricot and almond chutney

Coriander seeds and turmeric add a slightly spicy touch to this rich golden chutney. It is delicious in little canapés or with cubes of mozzarella cheese; it is also good in sandwiches.

Makes about 1.8kg/4lb

INGREDIENTS

1 small butternut squash, weighing about 800g/1¾lb

400g/14oz/2 cups golden granulated sugar

600ml/1 pint/2½ cups cider vinegar

2 onions, chopped

225g/8oz/1 cup ready-to-eat dried apricots, quartered

finely grated rind and juice of 1 orange

2.5ml/½ tsp turmeric

15ml/1 tbsp coriander seeds

15ml/1 tbsp salt

115g/4oz/1 cup flaked (sliced) almonds

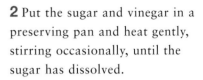

1 Halve the butternut squash lengthways and scoop out the seeds. Peel off the skin, then cut the flesh into 2cm/¾in cubes.

2 Put the sugar and vinegar in a preserving pan and heat gently, stirring occasionally, until the sugar has dissolved.

3 Add the squash, onions, apricots, orange rind and juice, turmeric, coriander seeds and salt to the preserving pan. Bring the mixture slowly to the boil.

4 Reduce the heat and simmer gently for 45–50 minutes, stirring frequently towards the end of the cooking time, until the chutney is reduced to a thick consistency and no excess liquid remains. Stir in the flaked almonds.

5 Spoon the chutney into warmed sterilized jars, cover and seal. Store in a cool, dark place and allow to mature for at least 1 month before eating. Use within 2 years. Once opened, store in the refrigerator and use within 2 months.

VARIATION

If butternut squash is unavailable, use a wedge of pumpkin weighing about 500g/1¼lb instead.

sweet and hot dried fruit chutney

This rich, thick and slightly sticky preserve of spiced dried fruit is a wonderful way to enliven cold roast turkey left over from Christmas or Thanksgiving dinners.

Makes about 1.5kg/3lb 6oz

INGREDIENTS

350g/12oz/1½ cups ready-to-eat
   dried apricots
225g/8oz/1⅓ cups dried dates,
   stoned (pitted)
225g/8oz/1⅓ cups dried figs
50g/2oz/⅓ cup glacé (candied)
   citrus peel
150g/5oz/1 cup raisins
50g/2oz/½ cup dried cranberries
120ml/4fl oz/½ cup cranberry juice
400ml/14fl oz/1⅔ cups cider vinegar
225g/8oz/1 cup demerara (raw) sugar
finely grated rind and juice of 1 lemon
5ml/1 tsp mixed spice (apple pie spice)
5ml/1 tsp ground coriander
5ml/1 tsp cayenne pepper
5ml/1 tsp salt

1 ▼ Roughly chop the dried apricots, dates, figs and citrus peel, then put all the dried fruit in a preserving pan. Pour over the cranberry juice, stir, then cover and leave to soak for 2 hours, or until the fruit has absorbed most of the juice.

2 Add the cider vinegar and sugar to the pan. Stir over a low heat until the sugar has dissolved.

3 Bring the mixture to the boil, then reduce the heat and simmer for about 30 minutes, or until the fruit is soft and the chutney fairly thick. Stir occasionally during cooking.

4 Stir in the lemon rind and juice, mixed spice, coriander, cayenne pepper and salt. Simmer for a further 15 minutes, stirring frequently towards the end of the cooking, until the chutney is thick and no excess liquid remains.

VARIATIONS

If you prefer, substitute dried sour cherries for the dried cranberries. Apple juice can be used instead of the cranberry juice.

5 Spoon the chutney into warmed sterilized jars, cover and seal. Store in a cool, dark place and allow to mature for at least 1 month before eating. Use within 1 year. Once opened, store in the refrigerator and use within 2 months.

pickled peach and chilli chutney

This is a spicy, rich chutney with a succulent texture. It is great served traditional-style, with cold roast meats such as ham, pork or turkey; it is also good with pan-fried chicken served in warm wraps. Try it with ricotta cheese as a filling for pitta bread.

Makes about 450g/1lb

INGREDIENTS

475ml/16fl oz/2 cups cider vinegar

275g/10oz/1¼ cups light muscovado (brown) sugar

225g/8oz/1⅓ cups dried dates, stoned (pitted) and finely chopped

5ml/1 tsp ground allspice

5ml/1 tsp ground mace

450g/1lb ripe peaches, stoned and cut into small chunks

3 onions, thinly sliced

4 fresh red chillies, seeded and finely chopped

4 garlic cloves, crushed

5cm/2in piece fresh root ginger, peeled and finely grated

5ml/1 tsp salt

1 Place the vinegar, sugar, dates, allspice and mace in a large pan and heat gently, stirring, until the sugar has dissolved. Bring to the boil, stirring occasionally.

2 Add the peaches, sliced onions, chopped chillies, crushed garlic, grated ginger and salt, and bring the mixture back to the boil, stirring occasionally.

3 Reduce the heat and simmer for 40–50 minutes, or until the chutney has thickened. Stir frequently to prevent the mixture sticking to the bottom of the pan.

4 Spoon the hot cooked chutney into warmed sterilized jars and seal immediately. When cold, store the jars in a cool, dark place and leave the chutney to mature for at least 2 weeks before eating. Use within 6 months.

COOK'S TIP

To test the consistency of the chutney before bottling, spoon a little of the mixture on to a plate; the chutney should hold its shape.

hot yellow plum chutney

It is well worth seeking out yellow plums to make this hot, fragrant chutney. They give it a slightly tart flavour and make it the perfect accompaniment to deep-fried Asian-style snacks such as spring rolls and wontons, or battered vegetables and shellfish.

Makes 1.3kg/3lb

INGREDIENTS

900g/2lb yellow plums, halved and stoned (pitted)

1 onion, finely chopped

7.5cm/3in piece fresh root ginger, peeled and grated

3 whole star anise

350ml/12fl oz/1½ cups white wine vinegar

225g/8oz/1 cup soft light brown sugar

5 celery sticks, thinly sliced

3 green chillies, seeded and finely sliced

2 garlic cloves, crushed

1 Put the halved plums, onion, ginger and star anise in a large pan and pour over half the white wine vinegar. Bring to the boil and simmer gently over a low heat for about 30 minutes, or until the plums have softened.

2 Stir the remaining vinegar, sugar, sliced celery, chillies and crushed garlic into the plum mixture. Cook very gently over a low heat, stirring frequently, until the sugar has completely dissolved.

3 Bring the mixture to the boil, then simmer for 45–50 minutes, or until thick, with no excess liquid. Stir frequently during the final stages of cooking to prevent the chutney sticking to the pan.

4 Spoon the plum chutney into warmed sterilized jars, then cover and seal immediately.

5 Store the chutney in a cool, dark place and allow to mature for at least 1 month before using. Use within 2 years.

COOK'S TIPS

• Once opened, store the chutney in the refrigerator and use within 3 months.

• Be sure to use jars with non-metallic lids to store the chutney.

mango chutney

No Indian meal would be complete without this classic chutney. Its gloriously sweet, tangy flavour complements the warm taste of Indian spices perfectly, but it is equally good scooped up on crispy fried poppadums. Mango chutney is also great served with chargrilled chicken, turkey or duck breasts; with potato wedges and soured cream; or spread on cheese on toast.

Makes about 1kg/2¼lb

INGREDIENTS

900g/2lb mangoes, halved, peeled
  and stoned
2.5ml/½ tsp salt
225g/8oz cooking apples, peeled
300ml/½ pint/1¼ cups distilled
  malt vinegar
200g/7oz/scant 1 cup demerara
  (raw) sugar
1 onion, chopped
1 garlic clove, crushed
10ml/2 tsp ground ginger

COOK'S TIPS

• Once opened, store the chutney
in the refrigerator and use within
3 months.
• When serving mango chutney with
crispy poppadums, also offer a
selection of other condiments such
as salty lime pickle, finely chopped
fresh onion salad and minty yogurt.

1 Using a sharp knife, slice the mango flesh into chunks and place in a large, non-metallic bowl. Sprinkle with salt and set aside while you prepare the apples.

2 Using a sharp knife, cut the apples into quarters, then remove and discard the cores and peel. Chop the flesh roughly.

3 Put the malt vinegar and sugar in a preserving pan and heat very gently, stirring occasionally, until the sugar has dissolved completely.

4 Add the mangoes, apple, onion, garlic and ginger to the pan and slowly bring the mixture to the boil, stirring occasionally.

5 Reduce the heat and simmer gently for about 1 hour, stirring frequently towards the end of the cooking time, until the chutney is reduced to a thick consistency and no excess liquid remains.

6 Spoon the chutney into warmed sterilized jars, cover and seal. Store in a cool, dark place and allow to mature for at least 2 weeks before eating. Use within 1 year of making.

VARIATION

To make a chutney with a fiery, spicy kick to serve with cheeses and cold meats, seed and finely slice two green chillies and stir into the chutney with the garlic and ginger.

chunky pear and walnut chutney

This chutney recipe is ideal for using up hard windfall pears. Its mellow flavour is excellent with cheese and also good with grains such as in pilaff or with tabbouleh.

Makes about 1.8kg/4lb

INGREDIENTS

1.2kg/2½lb firm pears

225g/8oz tart cooking apples

225g/8oz onions

450ml/¾ pint/scant 2 cups cider vinegar

175g/6oz/generous 1 cup sultanas
(golden raisins)

finely grated rind and juice
of 1 orange

400g/14oz/2 cups granulated sugar

115g/4oz/1 cup walnuts,
roughly chopped

2.5ml/½ tsp ground cinnamon

1 Peel and core the fruit, then chop into 2.5cm/1in chunks. Peel and quarter the onions, then chop into pieces the same size. Place in a preserving pan with the vinegar.

2 Slowly bring to the boil, then reduce the heat and simmer for 40 minutes, until the apples, pears and onions are tender, stirring the mixture occasionally.

3 Meanwhile, put the sultanas in a small bowl, pour over the orange juice and leave to soak.

4 Add the sugar, sultanas, and orange rind and juice to the pan. Gently heat until the sugar has dissolved, then simmer for 30–40 minutes, or until the chutney is thick and no excess liquid remains. Stir frequently towards the end of cooking to prevent the chutney sticking on the bottom of the pan.

5 Gently toast the walnuts in a non-stick pan over a low heat for 5 minutes, stirring frequently, until lightly coloured. Stir the nuts into the chutney with the cinnamon.

6 Spoon the chutney into warmed sterilized jars, cover and seal. Store in a cool, dark place and leave to mature for at least 1 month. Use within 1 year.

green grape chutney

A hint of lime heightens the fragrant grape flavour and complements the sweetness of this chutney. It is delicious warmed with a knob of butter and served with roast pork.

Makes 1.2kg/2½lb

INGREDIENTS

900g/2lb/6 cups seedless green grapes

900g/2lb tart cooking apples

450g/1lb/2¼ cups granulated sugar

450ml/¾ pint/scant 2 cups white
 wine vinegar

finely grated rind and juice
 of 1 lime

1.5ml/¼ tsp salt

COOK'S TIP

Once opened, store the chutney in the refrigerator and use within 1 month.

1 Halve the grapes if large, then peel, core and finely chop the apples. Put the fruit in a preserving pan with the sugar and vinegar and slowly bring to the boil.

2 Reduce the heat and simmer the chutney for about 45 minutes, or until the fruit is tender and the chutney fairly thick.

3 Stir the lime rind and juice and salt into the chutney and simmer for 15 minutes until the chutney is thick and no excess liquid remains.

4 Spoon the chutney into warmed sterilized jars, cover and seal. Store in a cool, dark place and leave to mature for at least 1 month before eating. Use within 18 months.

beetroot and orange preserve

With its vibrant red colour and rich earthy flavour, this distinctive chutney is good with salads as well as full-flavoured cheeses such as mature Cheddar, Stilton or Gorgonzola. You might also like to try it with cream cheese in baked potatoes.

Makes about 1.4kg/3lb

INGREDIENTS

350g/12oz raw beetroot (beets)

350g/12oz eating apples

300ml/½ pint/1¼ cups malt vinegar

200g/7oz/1 cup granulated sugar

225g/8oz red onions,
  finely chopped

1 garlic clove, crushed

finely grated rind and juice
  of 2 oranges

5ml/1 tsp ground allspice

5ml/1 tsp salt

1 Scrub or, if necessary, thinly peel the beetroot, then cut into 1cm/½in pieces. Peel, quarter and core the apples and cut into 1cm/½in pieces.

2 Put the vinegar and sugar in a preserving pan and heat gently, stirring occasionally, until the sugar has dissolved.

3 Add the beetroot, apples, onions, garlic, orange rind and juice, ground allspice and salt to the pan. Bring to the boil, reduce the heat, then simmer for 40 minutes.

4 Increase the heat slightly and boil for 10 minutes, or until the chutney is thick and no excess liquid remains. Stir frequently to prevent the chutney catching on the base of the pan.

5 Spoon the chutney into warmed sterilized jars, cover and seal. Store in a cool, dark place and allow to mature for at least 2 weeks before eating. Use within 6 months of making. Refrigerate once opened and use within 1 month.

COOK'S TIP

For speedy preparation and a fine-textured chutney, put the peeled beetroot through the coarse grating blade of a food processor.

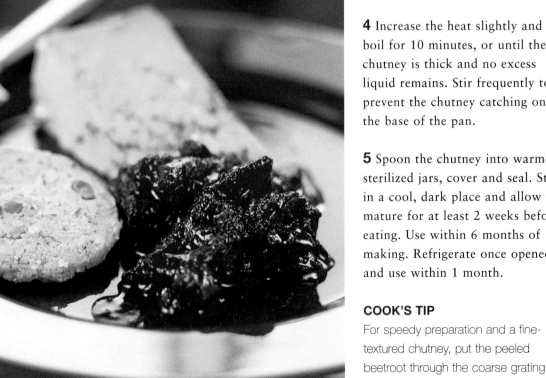

rhubarb and tangerine chutney

The rhubarb in this soft-textured chutney is added partway through the cooking, so that it retains its attractive colour and shape. It works especially well when partnered with Chinese-style roast duck, or with cold meats such as ham or gammon.

Makes about 1.3kg/3lb

INGREDIENTS

1 large onion, finely chopped

300ml/½ pint/1¼ cups distilled malt vinegar

4 whole cloves

7.5cm/3in cinnamon stick

1 tangerine

400g/14oz/2 cups granulated sugar

150g/5oz/1 cup sultanas (golden raisins)

1kg/2¼lb rhubarb, cut into 2.5cm/1in lengths

1 Put the onion in a preserving pan with the vinegar, whole cloves and cinnamon stick. Bring to the boil, then reduce the heat and simmer for 10 minutes, or until the onions are just tender.

2 Meanwhile, thinly pare the rind from the tangerine. (It is often easier to peel the fruit first, then slice the white pith from the rind.) Finely shred the rind.

3 Add the tangerine rind, sugar and sultanas to the pan. Stir until all the sugar has dissolved, then simmer for 10 minutes, or until the syrup is thick.

4 Add the rhubarb to the pan. Cook gently for about 15 minutes, stirring carefully from time to time, until the rhubarb is soft but still retains its shape, and just a little spare liquid remains.

5 Remove the pan from the heat and leave to cool for 10 minutes, then stir gently to distribute the fruit. Spoon the chutney into warmed sterilized jars, cover and seal. Store in a cool, dark place and allow to mature for at least 1 month. Use within 1 year. Once opened, store in the refrigerator and use within 2 months.

COOK'S TIP

The finely shredded rind of half an orange may be used in place of the shredded tangerine rind.

relishes

These versatile condiments can be fresh and quick to make or rich and slowly simmered. They usually have bold, striking flavours with a piquant, sharp and spicy taste balanced by sweet and tangy tones. Serve them with cheese, cold or grilled meats or use them to jazz up sandwich fillings.

tart tomato relish

Adding lime to this relish gives it a wonderfully tart, tangy flavour and a pleasantly sour after-taste. It is particularly good served with grilled or roast meats such as pork or lamb.

Makes about 500g/1¼lb

INGREDIENTS

2 pieces preserved stem ginger

1 lime

450g/1lb cherry tomatoes

115g/4oz/½ cup muscovado (molasses) sugar

120ml/4fl oz/½ cup white wine vinegar

5ml/1 tsp salt

VARIATION

Use chopped tomatoes in place of the cherry tomatoes, if you prefer.

1 Coarsely chop the preserved stem ginger. Slice the lime thinly, including the rind, then chop the slices into small pieces.

2 Place the cherry tomatoes, sugar, vinegar, salt, ginger and lime in a large heavy pan.

3 Bring the mixture to the boil, stirring until the sugar dissolves, then simmer rapidly for about 45 minutes. Stir frequently until the liquid has evaporated and the relish is thick and pulpy.

4 Leave the relish to cool for about 5 minutes, then spoon into sterilized jars. Leave to cool, then cover and store in the refrigerator for up to 1 month.

COOK'S TIP

There is always discussion between preserving enthusiasts as to the best choice of covering for chutneys and pickles. While cellophane covers are vinegarproof, they are difficult to secure for a good airtight seal, and not very good once opened. Screw-top lids with a plastic coating inside are best: put them on as soon as the piping hot preserve is potted and they will provide a hygienic, air-tight seal. New lids can be purchased for standard-size glass jars.

red hot relish

*Make this relish during the summer months when tomatoes and peppers are plentiful.
It enhances simple, plain dishes such as a cheese or mushroom omelette.*

Makes about 1.3kg/3lb

800g/1¾lb ripe tomatoes, skinned
and quartered

450g/1lb red onions, chopped

3 red (bell) peppers, seeded
and chopped

3 fresh red chillies, seeded
and finely sliced

200g/7oz/1 cup granulated sugar

200ml/7fl oz/scant 1 cup red
wine vinegar

30ml/2 tbsp mustard seeds

10ml/2 tsp celery seeds

15ml/1 tbsp paprika

5ml/1 tsp salt

1 Put the chopped tomatoes, onions, peppers and chillies in a preserving pan, cover with a lid and cook over a very low heat for about 10 minutes, stirring once or twice, until the tomato juices start to run.

2 Add the sugar and vinegar to the tomato mixture and slowly bring to the boil, stirring occasionally until the sugar has dissolved completely. Add the mustard seeds, celery seeds, paprika and salt and stir well to combine.

3 Increase the heat under the pan slightly and cook the relish, uncovered, for about 30 minutes, or until most of the liquid has evaporated and the mixture has a thick, but moist consistency. Stir frequently towards the end of cooking time to prevent the mixture sticking to the pan.

4 Spoon the relish into warmed sterilized jars, cover and seal. Store in a cool, dark place and leave to mature for at least 2 weeks before eating. Use the relish within 1 year of making.

COOK'S TIP

Once opened, store the relish in the refrigerator and use within 2 months.

bloody mary relish

This fresh-tasting relish with contrasting textures of tomatoes, celery and cucumber is perfect for al fresco *summer eating. For a special occasion, serve it with freshly shucked oysters.*

Makes about 1.3kg/3lb

INGREDIENTS

1.3kg/3lb ripe well-flavoured tomatoes
1 large cucumber
30–45ml/2–3 tbsp salt
2 celery sticks, chopped
2 garlic cloves, peeled and crushed
175ml/6fl oz/¾ cup white wine vinegar
15ml/1 tbsp granulated sugar
60ml/4 tbsp vodka
5ml/1 tsp Tabasco sauce
10ml/2 tsp Worcestershire sauce

COOK'S TIP

To skin the tomatoes, plunge them in a bowl of just-boiled water for 30 seconds. The skins will split and will be easy to peel off.

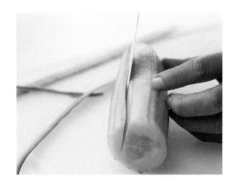

1 Skin and chop the tomatoes. Peel the cucumber and slice the flesh from around the seeds. Discard the seeds and chop the flesh. Layer the vegetables in a colander placed over a bowl, lightly sprinkling each layer with salt. Cover, put in the refrigerator and leave to drain overnight.

2 The next day, rinse the tomatoes and cucumber thoroughly under cold running water to remove as much salt as possible. Drain well, then place in a pan. Discard the salty vegetable juices in the bowl.

3 Add the celery, garlic, vinegar and sugar to the pan and slowly bring to the boil over a low heat.

4 Cook the vegetables, uncovered, for about 30 minutes, stirring occasionally, until the vegetables have softened and most of the liquid has evaporated.

5 Remove the pan from the heat and leave to cool for about 5 minutes. Add the vodka, and Tabasco and Worcestershire sauces and stir well to combine.

6 Spoon the hot relish into warmed sterilized jars, cool, cover and seal. Store in the refrigerator for at least 1 week.

COOK'S TIP

Use the relish within 3 months. Once opened, store it in the refrigerator and use within 1 month.

yellow pepper and coriander relish

Fresh relishes are quick and easy to make although they do not have a long shelf life. Try this relish with mild, creamy cheeses or with grilled tuna or other firm fish, poultry or meat.

Makes 1 small jar

INGREDIENTS

1 large yellow (bell) pepper
45ml/3 tbsp sesame oil
1 large mild fresh red chilli
small handful of fresh coriander (cilantro)
salt

1 Seed and coarsely chop the yellow peppers. Heat the oil in a pan, add the peppers and cook, stirring frequently, for 8–10 minutes, until lightly coloured.

2 Meanwhile, seed the chilli, slice it very thinly and set aside. Transfer the peppers to a food processor and process until chopped, but not puréed. Transfer half the peppers to a bowl, leaving the rest in the food processor.

3 Using a sharp knife, chop the fresh coriander, then add it to the mixture in the food processor and process briefly to combine. Tip the mixture into the bowl with the rest of the peppers, add the sliced chilli and stir well to combine.

4 Season the relish with salt to taste and stir well to combine. Cover the bowl with clear film (plastic wrap) and chill in the refrigerator until ready to serve.

COOK'S TIPS

• Red and orange sweet peppers work just as well as yellow, though green peppers are unsuitable as they are not sweet enough in flavour.

• This relish does not keep well, so use within 3 or 4 days of making.

• If you find the flavour of chilli too hot, use only half a chilli and chop into tiny pieces.

sweet piccalilli

Undoubtedly one of the most popular relishes, piccalilli can be eaten with grilled sausages, ham or chops, cold meats or a strong, well-flavoured cheese such as Cheddar. It should contain a good selection of fresh crunchy vegetables in a smooth, mustard sauce.

Makes about 1.8kg/4lb

INGREDIENTS

1 large cauliflower

450g/1lb pickling (pearl) onions

900g/2lb mixed vegetables, such as marrow (large zucchini), cucumber, French (green) beans

225g/8oz/1 cup salt

2.4 litres/4 pints/10 cups cold water

200g/7oz/1 cup granulated sugar

2 garlic cloves, peeled and crushed

10ml/2 tsp mustard powder

5ml/1 tsp ground ginger

1 litre/1¾ pints/4 cups distilled (white) vinegar

25g/1oz/¼ cup plain (all-purpose) flour

15ml/1 tbsp turmeric

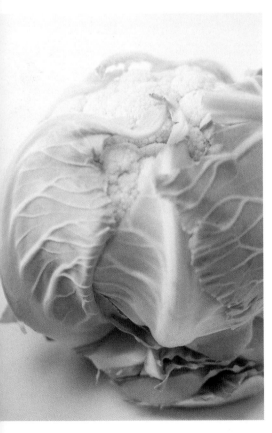

1 Prepare the vegetables. Divide the cauliflower into small florets; peel and quarter the pickling onions; seed and finely dice the marrow and cucumber; top and tail the French beans, then cut them into 2.5cm/1in lengths.

2 Layer the vegetables in a large glass or stainless steel bowl, generously sprinkling each layer with salt. Pour over the water, cover the bowl with clear film (plastic wrap) and leave to soak for about 24 hours.

3 Drain the soaked vegetables, and discard the brine. Rinse well in several changes of cold water to remove as much salt as possible, then drain them thoroughly.

4 Put the sugar, garlic, mustard, ginger and 900ml/1½ pints/3¾ cups of the vinegar in a preserving pan. Heat gently, stirring occasionally, until the sugar has dissolved.

5 Add the vegetables to the pan, bring to the boil, reduce the heat and simmer for 10–15 minutes, or until they are almost tender.

6 Mix the flour and turmeric with the remaining vinegar and stir into the vegetables. Bring to the boil, stirring, and simmer for 5 minutes, until the piccalilli is thick.

7 Spoon the piccalilli into warmed sterilized jars, cover and seal. Store in a cool, dark place for at least 2 weeks. Use within 1 year.

corn relish

When golden corn cobs are in season, try preserving their kernels in this delicious relish. It has a lovely crunchy texture and a wonderfully bright, appetizing appearance.

Makes about 1kg/2¼lb

INGREDIENTS

6 large fresh corn on the cob

½ small white cabbage, weighing about 275g/10oz, very finely shredded

2 small onions, halved and very finely sliced

475ml/16fl oz/2 cups distilled malt vinegar

200g/7oz/1 cup golden granulated sugar

1 red (bell) pepper, seeded and finely chopped

5ml/1 tsp salt

15ml/1 tbsp plain (all-purpose) flour

5ml/1 tsp mustard powder

2.5ml/½ tsp turmeric

1 Put the corn in a pan of boiling water and cook for 2 minutes. Drain and, when cool enough to handle, use a sharp knife to strip the kernels from the cobs.

2 Put the corn kernels in a pan with the cabbage and onions. Reserve 30ml/2 tbsp of the vinegar, then add the rest to the pan with the sugar. Slowly bring to the boil, stirring occasionally until the sugar dissolves. Simmer for 15 minutes. Add the red pepper and simmer for a further 10 minutes.

3 Blend the salt, flour, mustard and turmeric with the reserved vinegar to make a smooth paste.

4 Stir the paste into the vegetable mixture and bring back to the boil. Simmer for 5 minutes, until the mixture has thickened.

5 Spoon the relish into warmed sterilized jars, cover and seal. Store in a cool dark place. Use within 6 months of making. Once opened, store in the refrigerator and use within 2 months.

COOK'S TIP

This tangy relish is the perfect barbecue preserve. It is perfect for enlivening barbecued meats such as chicken, sausages and burgers.

cool cucumber and green tomato relish

This is a great way to use up those green tomatoes that seem as though they're never going to ripen. Combined with cucumber, they make a pale green relish that is great for barbecues.

Makes about 1.6kg/3½lb

INGREDIENTS

2 cucumbers

900g/2lb green tomatoes

4 onions

7.5ml/1½ tsp salt

350ml/12fl oz/1½ cups distilled (white) vinegar

150g/5oz/scant ¾ cup demerara (raw) sugar

200g/7oz/1 cup granulated sugar

15ml/1 tbsp plain (all-purpose) flour

2.5ml/½ tsp mustard powder

1 Wash the cucumbers and green tomatoes. Cut into 1cm/½in cubes. Peel and finely chop the onions.

2 Layer the vegetables in a strainer or colander placed over a bowl, lightly sprinkling each layer with salt, then cover and leave to drain for at least 6 hours, or overnight.

3 Discard the salty liquid and tip the salted vegetables into a large heavy pan. Reserve 30ml/2 tbsp of the vinegar and add the rest to the pan with the demerara and granulated sugars.

4 Slowly bring the vegetable mixture to the boil, stirring occasionally until the sugar has dissolved completely. Reduce the heat slightly and cook, uncovered, for about 30 minutes, or until the vegetables are tender.

5 In a small bowl, blend the flour and mustard to a paste with the reserved vinegar. Stir the mixture into the relish and simmer for about 20 minutes, or until the mixture is very thick.

6 Spoon the relish into warmed sterilized jars, cover and seal. Store in a cool, dark place for at least 1 week. Use the relish within 6 months. Once opened, keep in the refrigerator and use within 2 months.

carrot and almond relish

This is a Middle Eastern classic, usually made with long fine strands of carrot, available from many supermarkets. Alternatively, grate large carrots lengthways on a medium grater.

2 Put the lemon juice, vinegar, water, honey and salt in a jug (pitcher) and stir until the salt has dissolved. Pour over the carrot mixture. Mix well, cover and leave in the refrigerator for 4 hours.

3 Transfer the chilled mixture to a preserving pan. Slowly bring to the boil, then reduce the heat and simmer for 15 minutes until the carrots and ginger are tender.

4 Increase the heat and boil for 15 minutes, or until most of the liquid has evaporated and the mixture is thick. Stir frequently towards the end of the cooking time to prevent the mixture from sticking to the pan.

5 Put the almonds in a frying pan and toast over a low heat until just beginning to colour. Gently stir into the relish, taking care not to break the almonds.

Makes about 675g/1½lb

INGREDIENTS

15ml/1 tbsp coriander seeds

500g/1¼lb carrots, grated

50g/2oz fresh root ginger, finely shredded

200g/7oz/1 cup caster (superfine) sugar

finely grated rind and juice of 1 lemon

120ml/4fl oz/½ cup white wine vinegar

75ml/5 tbsp water

30ml/2 tbsp clear honey

7.5ml/1½ tsp salt

50g/2oz/½ cup flaked (sliced) almonds

1 Crush the coriander seeds using a mortar and pestle. Put them in a bowl with the carrots, ginger, sugar and lemon rind and mix together well to combine.

6 Spoon the relish into warmed sterilized jars, cover and seal. Leave for at least 1 month and use within 18 months. Once opened, store in the refrigerator.

lemon and garlic relish

This powerful relish is flavoured with North African spices and punchy preserved lemons, which are widely available in Middle Eastern stores. It is great served with Moroccan tagines.

Makes 1 small jar

INGREDIENTS

45ml/3 tbsp olive oil

3 large red onions, sliced

2 heads of garlic, separated into cloves and peeled

10ml/2 tsp coriander seeds, crushed

10ml/2 tsp light muscovado (brown) sugar, plus a little extra

pinch of saffron threads

5cm/2in piece cinnamon stick

2–3 small whole dried red chillies (optional)

2 fresh bay leaves

30–45ml/2–3 tbsp sherry vinegar

juice of ½ small orange

30ml/2 tbsp chopped preserved lemon

salt and ground black pepper

1 Gently heat the oil in a large heavy pan. Add the onions and stir, then cover and cook on the lowest setting for 10–15 minutes, stirring occasionally, until soft.

2 Add the garlic cloves and the coriander seeds. Cover and cook for 5–8 minutes, until soft.

3 Add a pinch of salt, lots of ground black pepper and the sugar to the onions and cook, uncovered, for a further 5 minutes.

4 Soak the saffron threads in about 45ml/3 tbsp warm water for 5 minutes, then add to the onions, with the soaking water. Add the cinnamon stick, dried chillies, if using, and bay leaves. Stir in 30ml/2 tbsp of the sherry vinegar and the orange juice.

5 Cook very gently, uncovered, until the onions are very soft and most of the liquid evaporated. Stir in the preserved lemon and cook gently for 5 minutes.

6 Taste the relish and adjust the seasoning, adding more salt, sugar and/or vinegar to taste.

7 Serve warm or cold (not hot or chilled). The relish tastes best if left to stand for 24 hours.

COOK'S TIP

You can store the relish in a tightly covered bowl or jar for up to a week in the refrigerator. Allow it to stand at room temperature for about an hour before serving.

cranberry and red onion relish

This wine-enriched relish is perfect for serving with hot roast turkey at Christmas or Thanksgiving. It is also good served with cold meats or stirred into a beef or game casserole for a touch of sweetness. It can be made several months in advance of the festive season.

Makes about 900g/2lb

INGREDIENTS

450g/1lb small red onions
30ml/2 tbsp olive oil
225g/8oz/1 cup soft light
  brown sugar
450g/1lb/4 cups fresh or
  frozen cranberries
120ml/4fl oz/½ cup red wine vinegar
120ml/4fl oz/½ cup red wine
15ml/1 tbsp mustard seeds
2.5ml/½ tsp ground ginger
30ml/2 tbsp orange liqueur or port
salt and ground black pepper

VARIATION

Redcurrants make a very good substitute for cranberries in this recipe. They produce a relish with a lovely flavour and pretty colour.

1 Halve the red onions and slice them very thinly. Heat the oil in a large pan, add the onions and cook them over a very low heat for about 15 minutes, stirring occasionally until softened. Add 30ml/2 tbsp of the sugar and cook for a further 5 minutes, or until the onions are caramelized.

2 Meanwhile, put the cranberries in a pan with the remaining sugar, and the vinegar, red wine, mustard seeds and ginger. Heat gently until the sugar has dissolved, then cover and bring to the boil.

3 Simmer the relish mixture for 12–15 minutes, until the berries have burst and are tender, then stir in the caramelized onions.

4 Increase the heat slightly and cook uncovered for a further 10 minutes, stirring the mixture frequently until it is well reduced and thickened. Remove the pan from the heat, then season with salt and pepper to taste.

5 Transfer the relish to warmed sterilized jars. Spoon a little of the orange liqueur or port over the top of each, then cover and seal. Store in a cool place for up to 6 months. Store in the refrigerator once opened and use within 1 month.

COOK'S TIP

It is important to cover the pan when cooking the cranberries because they can sometimes pop out of the pan during cooking and are very hot.

mango and papaya relish

Brightly coloured pieces of dried papaya adds taste and texture to this anise-spiced mango preserve. The fruit is cooked for only a short time to retain its juicy texture and fresh flavour.

Makes about 800g/1¾lb

INGREDIENTS

115g/4oz/½ cup dried papaya

30ml/2 tbsp orange or
    apple juice

2 large slightly underripe mangoes

2 shallots, very finely sliced

4cm/1½in piece fresh root
    ginger, grated

1 garlic clove, crushed

2 whole star anise

150ml/¼ pint/⅔ cup cider vinegar

75g/3oz/scant ½ cup light muscovado
    (brown) sugar

1.5ml/¼ tsp salt

1 Using a sharp knife or scissors, roughly chop the papaya and place in a small bowl. Sprinkle over the orange or apple juice and leave to soak for at least 10 minutes.

2 Meanwhile, peel and slice the mangoes, cutting the flesh away from the stone (pit) in large slices. Cut into 1cm/½in chunks, then set the flesh aside.

3 Put the sliced shallots, ginger, garlic and star anise in a large pan. Pour over the vinegar. Slowly bring to the boil, then reduce the heat, cover and simmer for 5 minutes, or until the shallots are just beginning to soften.

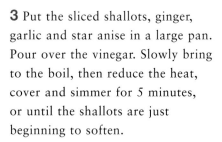

4 Add the sugar and salt to the pan and stir over a low heat until dissolved. When the mixture is simmering, add the papaya and mango and cook for a further 20 minutes, or until the fruit is just tender and the relish mixture has reduced and thickened.

5 Allow the relish to cool for about 5 minutes, then spoon into warmed sterilized jars. Allow to cool completely before covering and sealing. Store in a cool, dark place and use within 3 months of making. Once opened, keep the jars in the refrigerator and use within 1 month.

sweet and sour pineapple relish

This simple preserve is an excellent condiment for perking up grilled chicken or bacon chops. Using canned pineapple means it can be made mainly from store-cupboard ingredients.

Makes about 675g/1½lb

INGREDIENTS

2 x 400g/14oz cans pineapple rings or pieces in natural juice

1 lemon

115g/4oz/½ cup granulated sugar

45m/3 tbsp white wine vinegar

6 spring onions (scallions), finely chopped

2 fresh red chillies, seeded and finely chopped

salt and ground black pepper

1 Drain the pineapple, reserving 120ml/4fl oz/½ cup of the juice. Pour the juice into a preserving pan. Finely chop the pineapple, if necessary, and place in a sieve (strainer) set over a bowl.

2 Pare a strip of rind from the lemon. Squeeze the lemon juice and add to the pan with the lemon rind, sugar and vinegar.

3 Heat over a low heat, stirring occasionally, until the sugar has dissolved, then bring to the boil. Cook, uncovered, over a medium heat for about 10 minutes, or until the sauce has thickened slightly.

4 Add the chopped onions and chillies to the pan, together with any juice that has been drained from the chopped pineapple.

5 Cook the sauce for 5 minutes, until thick and syrupy, stirring frequently towards the end of the cooking time.

6 Increase the heat slightly, add the pineapple and cook for about 4 minutes, or until most of the liquid has evaporated. Season.

7 Spoon the relish into warmed sterilized jars, cover and seal. Store in the refrigerator and eat within 3 months of making.

plum and cherry relish

This simple sweet and sour fruity relish complements rich poultry, game or meat such as roast duck or grilled duck breasts. Sieve a few spoonfuls into a sauce or gravy to add fruity zest and flavour, as well as additional colour.

Makes about 350g/12oz

INGREDIENTS

350g/12oz dark-skinned red plums

350g/12oz/2 cups cherries

2 shallots, finely chopped

15ml/1 tbsp olive oil

30ml/2 tbsp dry sherry

60ml/4 tbsp red wine vinegar

15ml/1 tbsp balsamic vinegar

1 bay leaf

90g/3½oz/scant ½ cup demerara (raw) sugar

1 Halve and stone (pit) the plums, then roughly chop the flesh. Stone all the cherries.

2 Cook the shallots gently in the oil for 5 minutes, or until soft. Add the fruit, sherry, vinegars, bay leaf and sugar.

3 Slowly bring the mixture to the boil, stirring until the sugar has dissolved completely. Increase the heat and cook briskly for about 15 minutes, or until the relish is very thick and the fruit tender.

4 Remove the bay leaf and spoon the relish into warmed sterilized jars. Cover and seal. Store the relish in the refrigerator and use within 3 months.

nectarine relish

This sweet and tangy fruit relish goes very well with hot roast meats such as pork and game birds such as guinea fowl and pheasant. Make it while nectarines are plentiful and keep tightly covered in the refrigerator to serve for Christmas, or even to give as a seasonal gift.

Makes about 450g/1lb

INGREDIENTS

45ml/3 tbsp olive oil

2 Spanish (Bermuda) onions, thinly sliced

1 fresh green chilli, seeded and finely chopped

5ml/1 tsp finely chopped fresh rosemary

2 bay leaves

450g/1lb nectarines, stoned (pitted) and cut into chunks

150g/5oz/1 cup raisins

10ml/2 tsp crushed coriander seeds

350g/12oz/1½ cups demerara (raw) sugar

200ml/7fl oz/scant 1 cup red wine vinegar

1 Heat the oil in a large pan. Add the onions, chilli, rosemary and bay leaves. Cook, stirring frequently, for about 15 minutes, or until the onions are soft.

COOK'S TIP

Pots of this relish make a lovely gift. Store it in pretty jars and add a colourful label identifying the relish, and reminding the recipient that it should be stored in the refrigerator, and when it should be used by.

2 Add the nectarines, raisins, coriander seeds, sugar and vinegar to the pan, then slowly bring to the boil, stirring frequently.

3 Reduce the heat under the pan and simmer gently for 1 hour, or until the relish is thick and sticky. Stir occasionally during cooking, and more frequently towards the end of cooking time to prevent the relish sticking to the pan.

4 Spoon the relish into warmed, sterilized jars and seal. Leave the jars to cool completely, then store in the refrigerator. The relish will keep well in the refrigerator for up to 5 months.

savoury jellies

Although many of the jellies in this chapter contain sugar, they are all prepared as a condiment to serve with savoury foods such as meat, fish or cheese. Soft or firmly set, these interesting jellies are made from fruits and vegetables and usually have a tangy, sweet-and-sour taste. Many are flavoured with zesty citrus fruits and are spiked with herbs and spices to produce wonderful aromatic flavours. They really are a true gourmet treat – enjoy!

lemon grass and ginger jelly

This aromatic jelly is delicious with Asian-style roast meat and poultry such as Chinese crispy duck. It is also the perfect foil for rich fish, especially cold smoked trout or mackerel.

2 Put the chopped lemon grass in a preserving pan and pour over the water. Add the lemons and ginger. Bring to the boil, then reduce the heat, cover and simmer for 1 hour, or until the lemons are pulpy.

3 Pour the fruit and juices into a sterilized jelly bag suspended over a large bowl. Leave to drain for at least 3 hours, or until the juice stops dripping.

4 Measure the juice into the cleaned preserving pan, adding 450g/1lb/2¼ cups sugar for every 600ml/1 pint/2½ cups juice.

5 Heat the mixture gently, stirring occasionally, until the sugar has dissolved completely. Boil rapidly for about 10 minutes until the jelly reaches setting point (105°C/220°F). Remove from the heat.

6 Skim any scum off the surface using a slotted spoon, then pour the jelly into warmed sterilized jars, cover and seal. Store in a cool, dark place and use within 1 year. Once opened, keep in the refrigerator. Eat within 3 months.

Makes about 900g/2lb

INGREDIENTS

2 lemon grass stalks

1.5 litres/2½ pints/6¼ cups water

1.3kg/3lb lemons, washed and cut into small pieces

50g/2oz fresh root ginger, unpeeled, thinly sliced

about 450g/1lb/2¼ cups preserving or granulated sugar

1 Using a rolling pin, bruise the lemon grass, then chop roughly.

roasted red pepper and chilli jelly

The hint of chilli in this glowing red jelly makes it ideal for spicing up hot or cold roast meat, sausages or hamburgers. The jelly is also good stirred into sauces or used as a glaze for poultry.

Makes about 900g/2lb

INGREDIENTS

8 red (bell) peppers, quartered
  and seeded

4 fresh red chillies, halved and seeded

1 onion, roughly chopped

2 garlic cloves, roughly chopped

250ml/8fl oz/1 cup water

250ml/8fl oz/1 cup white wine vinegar

7.5ml/1½ tsp salt

450g/1lb/2¼ cups preserving
  or granulated sugar

25ml/1½ tbsp powdered pectin

1 Arrange the peppers, skin side up, on a rack in a grill (broiling) pan and grill (broil) until the skins blister and blacken.

2 Put the peppers in a polythene bag until they are cool enough to handle, then remove the skins.

3 Put the skinned peppers, chillies, onion, garlic and water in a food processor or blender and process to a purée. Press the purée through a nylon sieve set over a bowl, pressing hard with a wooden spoon, to extract as much juice as possible. There should be about 750ml/1¼ pints/3 cups.

4 Scrape the purée into a large stainless steel pan, then stir in the white wine vinegar and salt.

5 In a bowl, combine the sugar and pectin, then stir it into the pepper mixture. Heat gently, stirring, until the sugar and pectin have dissolved completely, then bring to a rolling boil. Cook the jelly, stirring frequently, for exactly 4 minutes, then remove the pan from the heat.

6 Pour the jelly into warmed, sterilized jars. Leave to cool and set, then cover, label and store.

tomato and herb jelly

This dark golden jelly is delicious served with roast and grilled meats, especially lamb. It is also great for enlivening tomato-based pasta sauces: stirring a couple of teaspoons of the jelly into sauces helps to heighten their flavour and counteract acidity.

Makes about 1.3kg/3lb

INGREDIENTS

1.8kg/4lb tomatoes

2 lemons

2 bay leaves

300ml/½ pint/1¼ cups cold water

250ml/8fl oz/1 cup malt vinegar

bunch of fresh herbs such as rosemary, thyme, parsley and mint, plus a few extra sprigs for the jars

about 900g/2lb/4½ cups preserving or granulated sugar

COOK'S TIP

Once you have opened a jar of this jelly, store it in the refrigerator and use within 3 months.

1 Wash the tomatoes and lemons well, then cut the tomatoes into quarters and the lemons into small pieces. Put the chopped tomatoes and lemons in a large heavy pan with the bay leaves and pour over the water and vinegar.

2 Add the herbs, either one herb or a mixture if preferred. (If you are using pungent woody herbs such as rosemary and thyme, use about six sprigs; if you are using milder leafy herbs such as parsley or mint, add about 12 large sprigs.)

3 Bring the mixture to the boil, then reduce the heat. Cover the pan with a lid and simmer for about 40 minutes, or until the tomatoes are very soft.

4 Pour the tomato mixture and all the juices into a sterilized jelly bag suspended over a large bowl. Leave to drain for about 3 hours, or until the juices stop dripping.

5 Measure the juice into the cleaned pan, adding 450g/1lb/ 2¼ cups sugar for every 600ml/ 1 pint/2½ cups juice. Heat gently, stirring, until the sugar dissolves. Boil rapidly for 10 minutes, to setting point (105°C/220°F), then remove from the heat. Skim off any scum.

6 Leave the jelly for a few minutes until a skin forms. Place a herb sprig in each warmed sterilized jar, then pour in the jelly. Cover and seal when cold. Store in a cool, dark place and use within 1 year.

apple, orange and cider jelly

A spoonful or two of this tangy amber jelly adds a real sparkle to a plate of cold meats, especially ham and pork or rich game pâtés. Tart cooking apples make the best-flavoured jelly, while the addition of cloves gives it a wonderfully warm, spicy taste and aroma.

Makes about 1.8kg/4lb

INGREDIENTS

1.3kg/3lb tart cooking apples

4 oranges

4 whole cloves

1.2 litres/2 pints/5 cups sweet cider

about 600ml/1 pint/2½ cups cold water

about 800g/1¾lb/4 cups preserving
 or granulated sugar

VARIATION

Replace some of the apples with crab apples for a more distinctive taste.

1 Wash and chop the apples and oranges, then put in a preserving pan with the cloves, cider and water to barely cover the fruit.

2 Bring the mixture to the boil, cover and simmer gently for 1 hour, stirring occasionally.

3 Pour the fruit and juices into a sterilized jelly bag suspended over a large bowl. Leave to drain for at least 4 hours, or overnight, until the juices stop dripping.

4 Measure the juice into the cleaned preserving pan, adding 450g/1lb/2¼ cups sugar for every 600ml/1 pint/2½ cups juice.

5 Heat the mixture gently stirring, until the sugar has dissolved. Boil rapidly for about 10 minutes until setting point is reached (105°C/220°F). Remove from the heat.

6 Skim any scum off the surface, then pour the jelly into warmed sterilized jars. Cover and seal. Store in a cool, dark place and use within 18 months. Once opened, store in the refrigerator and eat within 3 months.

quince and rosemary jelly

The amount of water needed for this jelly varies according to the ripeness of the fruit. For a good set, hard under-ripe quinces should be used as they contain the most pectin. If the fruit is soft and ripe, add a little lemon juice along with the water.

Makes about 900g/2lb

INGREDIENTS

900g/2lb quinces, cut into small pieces, with bruised parts removed

900ml–1.2 litres/1½–2 pints/ 3¾–5 cups water

lemon juice (optional)

4 large sprigs of fresh rosemary

about 900g/2lb/4½ cups preserving or granulated sugar

1 Put the chopped quinces in a large heavy pan with the water, using the smaller volume if the fruit is ripe and the larger volume plus lemon juice if it is hard.

2 Reserve a few small sprigs of rosemary, then add the rest to the pan. Bring to the boil, reduce the heat, cover with a lid and simmer gently until the fruit becomes pulpy.

3 Remove and discard all the rosemary sprigs. (Don't worry about any tiny leaves that have fallen off during cooking.) Pour the fruit and juices into a sterilized jelly bag suspended over a large bowl. Leave for 3 hours, or until the juices stop dripping.

4 Measure the drained juice into the cleaned pan, adding 450g/1lb/ 2¼ cups sugar for every 600ml/ 1 pint/2½ cups juice.

5 Heat the mixture gently over a low heat, stirring occasionally, until the sugar has dissolved completely. Bring to the boil, then boil rapidly for about 10 minutes until the jelly reaches setting point (105°C/220°F). Remove the pan from the heat.

6 Skim any scum from the surface using a slotted spoon, then leave the jelly to cool for a few minutes until a thin skin begins to form on the surface.

7 Place a sprig of rosemary in each warmed sterilized jar, then pour in the jelly. Cover and seal when cold. Store in a cool, dark place and use within 1 year. Once the jelly is opened, keep it in the refrigerator and use within 3 months.

minted gooseberry jelly

This classic, tart jelly is an ideal complement to roast lamb. Rather surprisingly, the gooseberry juice takes on a pinkish tinge during cooking so does not produce a green jelly as one would expect.

Makes about 1.2kg/2½lb

INGREDIENTS

1.3kg/3lb/12 cups gooseberries
1 bunch fresh mint
750ml/1¼ pints/3 cups cold water
400ml/14fl oz/1⅔ cups white wine vinegar
about 900g/2lb/4½ cups preserving or
   granulated sugar
45ml/3 tbsp chopped fresh mint

1 Place the gooseberries, mint and water in a preserving pan. Bring to the boil, reduce the heat, cover and simmer for about 30 minutes, until the gooseberries are soft. Add the vinegar and simmer uncovered for a further 10 minutes.

2 Pour the fruit and juices into a sterilized jelly bag suspended over a large bowl. Leave to drain for at least 3 hours, or until the juices stop dripping, then measure the strained juices back into the cleaned preserving pan.

3 Add 450g/1lb/2½ cups sugar for every 600ml/1 pint/2½ cups juice, then heat gently, stirring, until the sugar has dissolved. Bring to the boil and cook for 15 minutes, or to setting point (105°C/220°F). Remove the pan from the heat.

4 Skim any scum from the surface. Leave to cool until a thin skin forms, then stir in the mint.

5 Pour the jelly into warmed sterilized jars, cover and seal. Store and use within 1 year. Once opened, store in the refrigerator and eat within 3 months.

plum and apple jelly

Use dark red cooking plums, damsons or wild plums such as bullaces to offset the sweetness of this deep-coloured jelly. Its flavour complements rich roast meats such as lamb and pork.

Makes about 1.3kg/3lb

INGREDIENTS

900g/2lb plums
450g/1lb tart cooking apples
150ml/¼ pint/⅔ cup cider vinegar
750ml/1¼ pints/3 cups water
about 675g/1½lb/scant 3½ cups
   preserving or granulated sugar

COOK'S TIP

This jelly can be stored for up to 2 years. However, once opened, it should be stored in the refrigerator and eaten within 3 months.

1 Cut the plums in half along the crease, twist the two halves apart, then remove the stones (pits) and roughly chop the flesh. Chop the apples, including the cores and skins. Put the fruit in a large heavy pan with the vinegar and water.

2 Bring the mixture to the boil, reduce the heat, cover and simmer for 30 minutes or until the fruit is soft and pulpy.

3 Pour the fruit and juices into a sterilized jelly bag suspended over a large bowl. Leave to drain for at least 3 hours, or until the fruit juices stop dripping.

4 Measure the juice into the cleaned pan, adding 450g/1lb/ 2¼ cups sugar for every 600ml/ 1 pint/2½ cups juice.

5 Bring the mixture to the boil, stirring occasionally, until the sugar has dissolved, then boil rapidly for about 10 minutes, or until the jelly reaches setting point (105°C/220°F). Remove the pan from the heat.

6 Skim any scum from from the surface, then pour the jelly into warmed sterilized jars. Cover and seal while hot. Store in a cool, dark place and use within 2 years.

blackberry and sloe gin jelly

Although they have a wonderful flavour, blackberries are full of pips, so turning them into a deep-coloured jelly is a good way to make the most of this full-flavoured hedgerow harvest. This preserve is delicious served with richly flavoured roast meats such as lamb.

Makes about 1.3kg/3lb

INGREDIENTS

450g/1lb sloes (black plums)
600ml/1 pint/2½ cups cold water
1.8kg/4lb/16 cups blackberries
juice of 1 lemon
about 900g/2lb/4½ cups preserving
  or granulated sugar
45ml/3 tbsp gin

VARIATION

Sloes are much harder to come by than blackberries and you will usually need to find them growing in the wild. If you can't find sloes, use extra blackberries in their place.

1 Wash the sloes and prick with a fine skewer. Put them in a large heavy pan with the water and bring to the boil. Reduce the heat, cover and simmer for 5 minutes.

2 Briefly rinse the blackberries in cold water and add them to the pan with the lemon juice.

3 Bring the fruit mixture back to a simmer and cook gently for about 20 minutes, or until the sloes are tender and the blackberries very soft, stirring once or twice.

4 Pour the fruit and juices into a sterilized jelly bag suspended over a large bowl. Leave to drain for at least 4 hours or overnight, until the juices have stopped dripping.

5 Measure the fruit juice into the cleaned preserving pan, adding 450g/1lb/2¼ cups sugar for every 600ml/1 pint/2½ cups juice.

6 Heat the mixture gently, stirring occasionally, until the sugar has dissolved completely. Bring to the boil, then boil rapidly for about 10 minutes until the jelly reaches setting point (105°C/220°F). Remove the pan from the heat.

7 Skim off any scum from the surface of the jelly using a slotted spoon, then stir in the gin.

8 Pour the jelly into warmed sterilized jars, cover and seal. Store in a cool, dark place and use within 2 years. Once opened, keep the jelly in the refrigerator and eat within 3 months.

COOK'S TIP

Sloes bring a good level of pectin to the jelly. If all blackberries are used without sloes, select some under-ripe fruit and use preserving sugar with added pectin for a good set.

cranberry and claret jelly

The slight sharpness of cranberries makes this a superb jelly for serving with rich meats such as lamb or game. Together with claret, the cranberries give the jelly a beautiful deep red colour.

Makes about 1.2kg/2½lb

INGREDIENTS

900g/2lb/8 cups fresh or
  frozen cranberries

350ml/12fl oz/1½ cups water

about 900g//2lb/4½ cups preserving
  or granulated sugar

250ml/8fl oz/1 cup claret

COOK'S TIP

When simmering the cranberries, keep the pan covered until they stop "popping", as they can occasionally explode and jump out of the pan.

1 Wash the cranberries, if fresh, and put them in a large heavy pan with the water. Cover the pan and bring to the boil.

2 Reduce the heat under the pan and simmer for about 20 minutes, or until the cranberries are soft.

3 Pour the fruit and juices into a sterilized jelly bag suspended over a large bowl. Leave to drain for at least 3 hours or overnight, until the juices stop dripping.

4 Measure the juice and wine into the cleaned preserving pan, adding 400g/14oz/2 cups preserving or granulated sugar for every 600ml/ 1 pint/2½ cups liquid.

5 Heat the mixture gently, stirring occasionally, until the sugar has dissolved, then bring to the boil and boil rapidly for 10 minutes until the jelly reaches setting point (105°C/220°F). Remove the pan from the heat.

6 Skim any scum from the surface using a slotted spoon and pour the jelly into warmed sterilized jars. Cover and seal. Store in a cool, dark place and use within 2 years. Once opened, keep the jelly in the refrigerator and eat within 3 months.

red grape, plum and cardamom jelly

Enhance the flavour of roast beef and steaks with a spoonful of deep ruby-coloured jelly.
You may need to add a little pectin to the jelly to ensure you achieve a really good set.

Makes about 1.3kg/3lb

INGREDIENTS

1.8kg/4lb plums

450g/1lb/3 cups red grapes

15ml/1 tbsp cardamom pods

600ml/1 pint/2½ cups cold water

350–450ml/12fl oz–¾ pint/1½ cups–
   scant 2 cups pectin stock (optional)

about 1kg/2¼lb/5 cups preserving
   or granulated sugar

1 Cut the plums in half, then twist the two halves apart and remove the stone (pit). Roughly chop the flesh and halve the grapes. Remove the cardamom seeds from the pods and crush them in a mortar.

2 Put the fruit and cardamom seeds in a large heavy pan and pour over the water. Slowly bring to the boil, then simmer for about 30 minutes, or until very tender.

3 Check the pectin content of the fruit (see below); if it is low, stir the pectin stock into the fruit mixture and simmer for 5 minutes.

COOK'S TIP

To check the pectin content of the fruit, spoon 5ml/1 tsp of the juices into a glass. Add 15ml/1 tbsp of methylated spirits (denatured alcohol) and shake gently. After about a minute a clot should form. If the clot is large and jelly-like or if two or three smaller clots form, the pectin content should be sufficient for a set. If there are lots of small clots, or none at all, the pectin content is low and additional pectin will be needed.

4 Pour the fruit into a sterilized jelly bag suspended over a large bowl. Leave to drain for 3 hours, or until the juices stop dripping. Measure the juice into a clean pan, adding 450g/1lb/2¼ cups sugar for every 600ml/1 pint/2½ cups juice.

5 Heat the mixture gently, stirring occasionally, until the sugar has completely dissolved.

6 Bring the mixture to the boil, then boil rapidly for 10 minutes until setting point is reached (105°C/220°F). Remove the pan from the heat.

7 Skim off any scum from the surface, then pour the jelly into warmed sterilized jars, cover and seal. Store in a cool, dark place and use within 2 years. Keep in the refrigerator once opened, and eat within 3 months.

pear and pomegranate jelly

This delicate jelly has a faintly exotic perfume. Pears are not naturally rich in pectin so liquid pectin needs to be added to the jelly during cooking to help it achieve a good set.

4 While the pears are simmering, cut the pomegranates in half horizontally, and use a lemon squeezer to extract all the juice: there should be about 250ml/ 8fl oz/1 cup.

5 Add the pomegranate juice to the pan and bring back to the boil. Reduce the heat and simmer for 2 minutes. Pour the fruit and juices into a sterilized jelly bag suspended over a large bowl. Leave to drip for at least 3 hours.

6 Measure the strained juice into the cleaned pan, adding 450g/1lb/ 2¼ cups sugar for every 600ml/ 1 pint/2½ cups juice.

7 Heat gently, stirring occasionally, until the sugar has dissolved. Bring to the boil, then boil rapidly for 3 minutes. Remove the pan from the heat and stir in the liquid pectin.

8 Skim any scum from the surface, then stir in the rose water, if using. Pour the jelly into warmed sterilized jars. Cover and seal. Store in a cool, dark place and use within 18 months.

Makes about 1.2kg/2½lb

INGREDIENTS

900g/2lb pears

pared rind and juice of 2 lemons

1 cinnamon stick

750ml/1¼ pints/3 cups water

900g/2lb red pomegranates

about 900g/2lb/4½ cups preserving or granulated sugar

250ml/8fl oz/1 cup liquid pectin

15ml/1 tbsp rose water (optional)

COOK'S TIP

Once opened, store the jelly in the refrigerator and use within 3 months.

1 Wash and remove the stalks from the pears and chop the fruit roughly. Put the chopped fruit in a large heavy pan with the lemon rind and juice, cinnamon stick and measured water.

2 Bring the mixture to the boil, then reduce the heat to low, cover with a lid and simmer gently for about 15 minutes.

3 Remove the lid from the pan, stir the fruit mixture, then leave to simmer, uncovered, for a further 15 minutes.

guava jelly

Fragrant guava makes an aromatic, pale rust-coloured jelly with a soft set and a slightly sweet-sour flavour that is enhanced by lime juice. Guava jelly goes well with goat's cheese.

Makes about 900g/2lb

INGREDIENTS

900g/2lb guavas
juice of 2–3 limes
about 600ml/1 pint/2½ cups cold water
about 500g/1¼lb/2½ cups preserving
 or granulated sugar

1 Thinly peel and halve the guavas. Using a spoon, scoop out the seeds (pips) from the centre of the fruit and discard them.

2 Place halved guavas in a large heavy pan with 15ml/1 tbsp lime juice and the water – there should be just enough to cover the fruit. Bring the mixture to the boil, then reduce the heat, cover with a lid and simmer for 30 minutes, or until the fruit is tender.

3 Pour the fruit and juices into a sterilized jelly bag suspended over a large bowl. Leave to drain for at least 3 hours.

COOK'S TIP

Do not be tempted to squeeze the jelly bag while the fruit juices are draining from it; this will result in a cloudy jelly.

4 Measure the juice into the cleaned preserving pan, adding 400g/14oz/2 cups sugar and 15ml/ 1 tbsp lime juice for every 600ml/ 1 pint/2½ cups guava juice.

5 Heat gently, stirring occasionally, until the sugar has dissolved. Boil rapidly for about 10 minutes. When the jelly reaches setting point, remove the pan from the heat.

6 Skim any scum from the surface of the jelly using a slotted spoon, then pour the jelly into warmed sterilized jars. Cover and seal.

7 Store the jelly in a cool, dark place and use within 1 year. Once opened, keep in the refrigerator and eat within 3 months.

sauces and mustards

No store cupboard is complete without a bottle of tangy sauce and a jar of peppery mustard for serving with hot and cold meats, spreading over cheese on toast, or smearing in a sandwich for an extra spicy bite. Mustard is also indispensable for enlivening mild sauces and dressings – even the smallest spoonful can completely transform a plain cheese sauce or a simple vinaigrette.

sherried plum sauce

Here, plums are cooked with their skins, then strained to make a smooth sauce. Sharp cooking plums, damsons or bullaces give the best flavour and help counteract the sweetness of the sauce, which is wonderful served with roast duck or goose.

2 Roughly chop the flesh and put in a large, heavy pan. If you're using damsons or bullaces, you may find it easier simply to chop them, leaving in the stones. Stir in the sherry and vinegar.

3 Slowly bring the mixture to the boil, then cover and cook over a gentle heat for about 10 minutes, or until the plums are very soft. Push the fruit through a food mill or sieve to remove the skins.

4 Return the plum purée to the pan and add the sugar, garlic, salt and ginger. Stir until the sugar has dissolved, then bring back to the boil and simmer uncovered for about 15 minutes, until thickened.

5 Remove the pan from the heat and stir in the Tabasco sauce. Ladle the sauce into hot sterilized jars. Add 5–10ml/1–2 tsp sherry to the top of each jar, then cover and seal. The sauce will keep for several weeks in the refrigerator or, if heat treated, for 6 months. Once opened, store in the refrigerator and use within 3 weeks.

Makes about 400ml/14fl oz/1⅔ cups

INGREDIENTS

450g/1lb dark plums or damsons

120ml/4fl oz/½ cup dry sherry, plus extra

30ml/2 tbsp sherry vinegar

175g/6oz/scant 1 cup light muscovado (brown) sugar

1 garlic clove, crushed

1.5ml/¼ tsp salt

2.5cm/1in piece fresh root ginger, finely chopped

3–4 drops of Tabasco sauce

1 Cut each plum in half, then twist apart and remove the stone (pit).

cumberland sauce

This sauce is thought to have been named after the Duke of Cumberland who became ruler of Hanover at a time when fruit sauces were served with meat and game in Germany. It goes well with cold cuts, pâtés and terrines, and Christmas or Thanksgiving turkey.

Makes about 750ml/1¼ pints/3 cups

INGREDIENTS

4 oranges
2 lemons
450g/1lb redcurrant or rowan jelly
150ml/¼ pint/⅔ cup port
20ml/4 tsp cornflour (cornstarch)
pinch of ground ginger

1 Scrub the oranges and lemons, then remove the rind thinly, paring away any white pith.

2 Cut the orange and lemon rind into very thin matchstick strips. Put the strips in a heavy pan, cover them with cold water and bring the water to the boil.

3 Simmer the rind for 2 minutes, then drain, cover with cold water, bring to the boil and simmer for about 3 minutes. Drain well and return the rind to the pan.

4 Squeeze the juice from the fruits, then add it to the pan with the redcurrant or rowan jelly. Reserve 30ml/2 tbsp of the port and add the rest to the pan.

5 Slowly bring the mixture to the boil, stirring until the jelly has melted. Simmer for 10 minutes until slightly thickened. Blend the cornflour and ginger with the reserved port and stir into the sauce. Cook over a low heat, stirring until the sauce thickens and boils. Simmer for 2 minutes.

6 Leave the sauce to cool for about 5 minutes, then stir again briefly. Pour into warmed sterilized wide-necked bottles or jars, cover and seal. The sauce will keep for several weeks in the refrigerator or, if heat treated, for 6 months. Once opened, store in the refrigerator and use within 3 weeks.

mint sauce

In England, mint sauce is the traditional and inseparable accompaniment to roast lamb. Its fresh, tart, astringent flavour is the perfect foil to rich, strongly flavoured lamb. It is extremely simple to make and is infinitely preferable to the ready-made varieties.

Makes about 250ml/8fl oz/1cup

INGREDIENTS

1 large bunch mint
105ml/7 tbsp boiling water
150ml/¼ pint/⅔ cup wine vinegar
30ml/2 tbsp granulated sugar

COOK'S TIP

To make a quick and speedy Indian raita for serving with crispy poppadums, simply stir a little mint sauce into a small bowl of natural (plain) yogurt. Serve the raita alongside a bowl of tangy mango chutney.

1 Using a sharp knife, chop the mint very finely and place it in a 600ml/1 pint/2½ cup jug (pitcher). Pour the boiling water over the mint and leave to infuse for about 10 minutes.

2 When the mint infusion has cooled and is lukewarm, stir in the wine vinegar and sugar. Continue stirring (but do not mash up the mint leaves) until the sugar has dissolved completely.

3 Pour the mint sauce into a sterilized bottle or jar, seal and store in the refrigerator.

COOK'S TIP

This mint sauce can keep for up to 6 months stored in the refrigerator, but is best used within 3 weeks.

traditional horseradish sauce

Fiery, peppery horseradish sauce is without doubt the essential accompaniment to roast beef and is also delicious served with smoked salmon. Horseradish, like chillies, is a powerful ingredient so you should take care when handling it and wash your hands straight afterwards.

Makes about 200ml/7fl oz/scant 1 cup

INGREDIENTS

45ml/3 tbsp freshly grated
   horseradish root
15ml/1 tbsp white wine vinegar
5ml/1 tsp granulated sugar
pinch of salt
150ml/¼ pint/⅔ cup thick double
   (heavy) cream, for serving

COOK'S TIP

To counteract the potent fumes of the horseradish, keep the root submerged in water while you chop and peel it. Use a food procssor to do the fine chopping or grating, and avert your head when removing the lid.

1 Place the grated horseradish in a bowl, then add the white wine vinegar, granulated sugar and just a pinch of salt.

2 Stir the ingredients together until thoroughly combined.

3 Pour the mixture into a sterilized jar. It will keep in the refrigerator for up to 6 months.

4 A few hours before you intend to serve the sauce, stir the cream into the horseradish and leave to infuse.

tangy tomato ketchup

Sweet, tangy, spicy tomato ketchup is perfect for serving with barbecued or grilled burgers and sausages. This home-made variety is so much better than store-bought tomato ketchup.

Makes about 1.3kg/3lb

INGREDIENTS

2.25kg/5lb very ripe tomatoes

1 onion

6 cloves

4 allspice berries

6 black peppercorns

1 fresh rosemary sprig

25g/1oz fresh root ginger, sliced

1 celery heart

30ml/2 tbsp soft light brown sugar

65ml/4½ tbsp raspberry vinegar

3 garlic cloves, peeled

15ml/1 tbsp salt

2 Tie the onion with the allspice, peppercorns, rosemary and ginger into a double layer of muslin (cheesecloth) and add to the pan. Chop the celery, plus the leaves, and add to the pan with the sugar, raspberry vinegar, garlic and salt.

3 Bring the mixture to the boil over a fairly high heat, stirring occasionally. Reduce the heat and simmer for 1½–2 hours, stirring regularly, until reduced by half. Purée the mixture in a food processor, then return to the pan, bring to the boil and simmer for 15 minutes. Bottle in clean, sterilized jars and store in the refrigerator. Use within 2 weeks.

1 Carefully peel and seed the ripe tomatoes, then chop and place in a large pan. Peel the onion, leaving the tip and root intact and stud it with the cloves.

barbecue sauce

As well as enlivening burgers and other food cooked on the barbecue, this sauce is also good for all manner of grilled meats and savoury pastries.

Makes about 900ml/1½ pints/3¾ cups

INGREDIENTS

30ml/2 tbsp olive oil

1 large onion, chopped

1 garlic clove, crushed

1 fresh red chilli, seeded and sliced

2 celery sticks, sliced

1 large carrot, sliced

1 medium cooking apple, quartered, cored, peeled and chopped

450g/1lb ripe tomatoes, quartered

2.5ml/½ tsp ground ginger

150ml/¼ pint/⅔ cup malt vinegar

1 bay leaf

4 whole cloves

4 black peppercorns

50g/2oz/¼ cup soft light brown sugar

10ml/2 tsp English mustard

2.5ml/½ tsp salt

1 Heat the oil in a large heavy pan. Add the onion and cook over a low heat for 5 minutes.

2 Stir in the garlic, chilli, celery and carrot into the onions and cook for 5 minutes, stirring frequently, until the onion just begins to colour.

3 Add the apple, tomatoes, ground ginger and malt vinegar to the pan and stir to combine.

4 Put the bay leaf, cloves and peppercorns on a square of muslin (cheesecloth) and tie into a bag with fine string. Add to the pan and bring to the boil. Reduce the heat, cover and simmer for about 45 minutes, stirring occasionally.

5 Add the sugar, mustard and salt to the pan and stir until the sugar dissolves. Simmer for 5 minutes. Leave to cool for 10 minutes, then remove the bag and discard.

6 Press the mixture through a sieve and return to the cleaned pan. Simmer for 10 minutes, or until thickened. Adjust the seasoning.

7 Pour the sauce into hot sterilized bottles or jars, then seal. Heat process, cool and, if using cork-topped bottles, dip the corks in wax. Store in a cool, dark place and use within 1 year. Once opened, store in the refrigerator and use within 2 months.

roasted red pepper and chilli ketchup

Roasting the peppers gives this ketchup a richer, smoky flavour. You can add fewer or more chillies according to taste. Once opened, store in the refrigerator and use within 3 months.

Makes about 600ml/1 pint/2½ cups

INGREDIENTS

900g/2lb red (bell) peppers

225g/8oz shallots

1 tart cooking apple, quartered, cored and roughly chopped

4 fresh red chillies, seeded and chopped

1 large sprig each thyme and parsley

1 bay leaf

5ml/1 tsp coriander seeds

5ml/1 tsp black peppercorns

600ml/1 pint/2½ cups water

350ml/12fl oz/1½ cups red wine vinegar

50g/2oz/scant ¼ cup granulated sugar

5ml/1 tsp salt

7.5ml/1½ tsp arrowroot

1 Preheat the grill (broiler). Place the red peppers on a baking sheet and grill for 10–12 minutes, turning them regularly, until the skins have blackened. Put the peppers in a plastic bag and leave for 5 minutes.

2 When the peppers are cool enough to handle, peel away the skin. To catch any remaining bits of skin, scrape the pepper with a knife, then quarter the peppers and remove the seeds. Roughly chop the flesh and place in a large pan.

3 Put the shallots in a bowl, pour over boiling water and leave to stand for 3 minutes. Drain the shallots, then rinse under cold water and peel. Chop the shallots and add to the pan with the apple and chillies.

4 Tie the thyme, parsley, bay leaf, coriander and peppercorns together in a square of muslin (cheesecloth).

5 Add the bag of herbs and the water to the pan and bring to the boil. Reduce the heat, cover and simmer for 30 minutes. Leave to cool for 15 minutes, then remove and discard the muslin bag.

6 Purée the mixture in a food processor, then press it through a sieve (strainer) and return the purée to the cleaned pan. Reserve 15ml/ 1 tbsp of the vinegar and add the rest to the pan with the sugar and salt.

7 Bring to the boil, stirring until the sugar has dissolved, then simmer for 45 minutes, or until the sauce is well reduced. Blend the arrowroot with the reserved vinegar, stir into the sauce, then simmer for 2–3 minutes, or until slightly thickened.

8 Pour the sauce into hot sterilized bottles, then seal, heat process and store in a cool, dark place and use within 18 months.

clove-spiced mustard

This spicy mustard is the perfect accompaniment to robust red meats such as sausages and steaks, particularly when they are cooked on the barbecue.

Makes about 300ml/½ pint/1¼ cups

INGREDIENTS

75g/3oz/scant ½ cup white
 mustard seeds

50g/2oz/¼ cup soft light brown sugar

5ml/1 tsp salt

5ml/1 tsp black peppercorns

5ml/1 tsp cloves

5ml/1 tsp turmeric

200ml/7fl oz/scant 1 cup distilled
 malt vinegar

COOK'S TIP

Cloves add a lovely, warming taste to this mustard. Make sure you use whole cloves in this mustard – ground cloves tend to have less flavour.

1 Put all the ingredients except the malt vinegar into a food processor or blender and process. Gradually add the vinegar, 15ml/1 tbsp at a time, processing well between each addition. Continue processing the mustard until it forms a fairly thick, coarse paste.

2 Leave the mustard to stand for 10–15 minutes to thicken slightly. Spoon into a 300ml/½ pint/1¼ cup sterilized jar or several smaller jars, using a funnel. Cover the surface with a greaseproof (waxed) paper disc, then seal with a screw-top lid or a cork, and label.

moutarde aux fines herbes

This classic, fragrant mustard may be used either as a delicious condiment or for coating meats such as chicken and pork, or oily fish such as mackerel, before cooking. It is also fabulous smeared thinly on cheese on toast for an added bite.

Makes about 300ml/½ pint/1¼ cups

INGREDIENTS

75g/3oz/scant ½ cup white mustard seeds

50g/2oz/¼ cup soft light brown sugar

5ml/1 tsp salt

5ml/1 tsp whole peppercorns

2.5ml/½ tsp ground turmeric

200ml/7fl oz/scant 1 cup distilled malt vinegar

60ml/4 tbsp chopped fresh mixed herbs, such as parsley, sage, thyme and rosemary

COOK'S TIP

Stir a spoonful of this fragrant mustard into creamy savoury sauces and salad dressings to enhance their flavour.

1 Put the mustard seeds, sugar, salt, whole peppercorns and ground turmeric into a food processor or blender and process for about 1 minute, or until the peppercorns are coarsely chopped.

2 Gradually add the vinegar to the mustard mixture, 15ml/1 tbsp at a time, processing well between each addition, then continue processing until a coarse paste forms.

3 Add the chopped fresh herbs to the mustard and mix well, then leave to stand for 10–15 minutes until the mustard thickens slightly.

4 Spoon the mustard into a 300ml/ ½ pint/1¼ cup sterilized jar. Cover the surface of the mustard with a greaseproof (waxed) paper disc, then seal with a screw-top lid or a cork, and label. Store in a cool, dark place.

honey mustard

Delicious home-made mustards mature to make the most aromatic of condiments. This honey mustard is richly flavoured and is wonderful served with meats and cheeses or stirred into sauces and salad dressings to give an extra, peppery bite. The addition of honey gives the mustard a deliciously rounded, full, slightly sweet flavour.

Makes about 500g/1¼lb

INGREDIENTS

225g/8oz/1 cup mustard seeds

15ml/1 tbsp ground cinnamon

2.5ml/½ tsp ground ginger

300ml/½ pint/1¼ cups white wine vinegar

90ml/6 tbsp dark clear honey

COOK'S TIP

Make sure you use well-flavoured clear, runny honey for this recipe. Set (crystallized) honey does not have the right consistency and will not work well.

1 Put the mustard seeds in a bowl with the spices and pour over the vinegar. Stir well to mix, then leave to soak overnight.

2 The next day, put the mustard mixture in a mortar and pound with a pestle, adding the honey very gradually.

3 Continue pounding and mixing until the mustard resembles a stiff paste. If the mixture is too stiff, add a little extra vinegar to achieve the desired consistency.

4 Spoon the mustard into four sterilized jars, seal and label, then store in the refrigerator and use within 4 weeks.

COOK'S TIP

This sweet, spicy mustard is perfect for adding extra flavour to cheese tarts or quiches. Spread a very thin layer of mustard across the base of the pastry case before adding the filling, then bake according to the recipe. The mustard will really complement the cheese, giving a mouth-watering result.

spiced tamarind mustard

Tamarind has a distinctive sweet and sour flavour, a dark brown colour and sticky texture. Combined with spices and ground mustard seeds, it makes a wonderful condiment.

Makes about 200g/7oz

INGREDIENTS

115g/4oz tamarind block

150ml/¼ pint/⅔ cup warm water

50g/2oz/¼ cup yellow mustard seeds

25ml/1½ tbsp black or brown
  mustard seeds

10ml/2 tsp clear honey

pinch of ground cardamom

pinch of salt

COOK'S TIP

The mustard will be ready to eat in 3–4 days. It should be stored in a cool, dark place and used within 4 months.

1 Put the tamarind in a small bowl and pour over the water. Leave to soak for 30 minutes. Mash to a pulp with a fork, then strain through a fine sieve into a bowl.

2 Grind the mustard seeds in a spice mill or coffee grinder and add to the tamarind with the remaining ingredients. Spoon into sterilized jars, cover and seal.

INDEX

A

almonds: butternut, apricot and almond
  chutney, 38
  carrot and almond relish, 58
apples
  apple, orange and cider jelly, 72
  fiery bengal chutney, 37
  kashmir chutney, 36
  plum and apple jelly, 75
apricots
  butternut, apricot and almond
    chutney, 38
aubergines
  mediterranean chutney, 34
  stuffed baby aubergines, 20

B

beetroot
  and orange preserve, 46
  pickled turnips and beetroot, 17
bell peppers see peppers
Bengal chutney, fiery, 37
berries see individual berries
blackberry and sloe gin jelly, 76
Bloody Mary relish, 52
bottles, 9, 11

C

cabbages
  pickled red, 16

canelle knives, 9
cardamom: red grape, plum and
  cardamom jelly, 79
carrot and almond relish, 58
cauliflower
  sweet piccalilli, 54
celery
  Bloody Mary relish, 52
cherries
  plum and cherry relish, 64
chillies
  pickled peach and chilli chutney, 40
  roasted red pepper and chilli jelly, 69
  roasted red pepper and chilli ketchup, 90
chutneys, 32–4, 36–42, 42–3, 47
  fiery Bengal chutney, 37
  Kashmir chutney, 36
  Mediterranean chutney, 34
  see also under separate ingredients
cider: apple, orange and cider jelly, 72
cilantro see coriander
claret: cranberry and claret jelly, 78
cloves
  clove-spiced mustard, 91
colanders, 9
coriander, yellow pepper and coriander
  relish, 53
corn relish, 56
courgettes
  Mediterranean chutney, 34
covering preserves, 11
cranberries
  and claret jelly, 78
  and red onion relish, 60
cucumbers
  Bloody Mary relish, 52
  cool cucumber and green tomato
    relish, 57
  dill pickles, 14

D

dill
  dill pickles, 14
dried fruits
  sweet and hot chutney, 39

E

eggplants see aubergines
equipment, 8–9

F

fruit: Italian mustard fruit pickles, 28
  see also individual fruits

G

garlic
  lemon and garlic relish, 59
  pickled mushrooms with, 15
gin: blackberry and sloe gin jelly, 76
ginger, lemon grass and ginger jelly, 68
gooseberries
  minted gooseberry jelly, 75
grapes
  green grape chutney, 45
  red grape, plum and cardamom
    jelly, 79
guavas, guava jelly, 81

H

herbs
  moutarde aux fines herbes, 92
  tomato and herb jelly, 70
history of preserving, 6–7
honey mustard, 92
horseradish sauce, 87
hydrometer, 9

K

ketchup
 roasted red pepper and chilli, 90
 tomato ketchup, 88

L

lemon and garlic relish, 59

M

mango
 mango chutney, 42
 mango and papaya relish, 62

N

nectarine relish, 65

O

onions
 confit of slow-cooked, 35
 cranberry and red onion relish, 60
 English pickled, 19
oranges
 apple, orange and cider jelly, 72
 beetroot and orange preserve, 46
 Cumberland sauce, 85
 striped, spiced, 26

P

papayas
 mango and papaya relish, 62
peaches
 pickled peach and chilli chutney, 40

pears
 blushing pears, 29
 chunky pear and walnut chutney, 44
 pear and pomegranate jelly, 80
peppers
 Mediterranean chutney, 34
 red hot relish, 51
 roasted red pepper and chilli jelly, 69
 roasted red pepper and chilli ketchup, 90
 yellow pepper and coriander relish, 53
pickles, 14–29
pineapples
 sweet and sour pineapple relish, 63
plums
 hot yellow plum chutney, 41
 pickled plums, 24
 plum and apple jelly, 75
 plum and cherry relish, 64
 red grape, plum and cardamom jelly, 79
 sherried plum sauce, 84
pomegranates
 pear and pomegranate jelly, 80
potting and covering preserves, 10–11

Q

quinces and rosemary jelly, 73

R

redcurrants
 Cumberland sauce, 85
relishes, 50–65
rhubarb and tangerine chutney, 47
rosemary, quince and rosemary jelly, 73

S

salometer, 9
sauces, 84–90
 barbecue sauce, 89
scallions see spring onions
shallots in balsamic vinegar, 18
sherry vinegar: sherried plum
 sauce, 84
sieves, 9
spiced tamarind mustard, 94
squashes
 butternut, apricot and almond
 chutney, 38

sterilizing jars and bottles, 10
storing preserves, 11

T

tangerines
 rhubarb and tangerine chutney, 47
tomatoes
 Bloody Mary relish, 52
 cool cucumber and green tomato
 relish, 57
 green tomato chutney, 32
 red hot relish, 51
 tart tomato relish, 50
 tomato chutney, 33
 tomato and herb jelly, 70
 tomato ketchup, 88
turnips
 pickled turnips and beetroot, 17

V

vegetables
 Mediterranean chutney, 34
 sweet piccalilli, 54
 see also individual types of vegetables

W

walnuts: chunky pear and
 walnut chutney, 44

Z

zesters, 9
zucchini see courgettes